FIFTY-FIFTY

A speaking and listening course

BOOK TWO

Third Edition

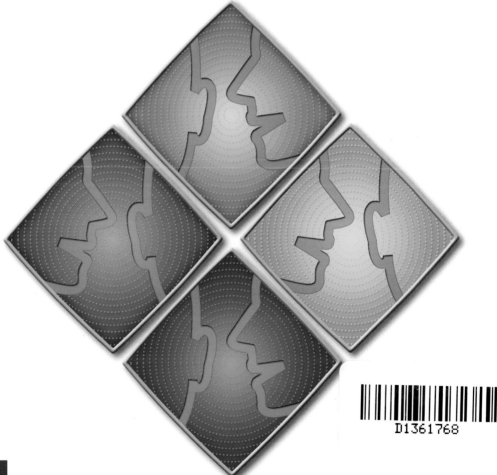

D1361768

PEARSON
Longman

WARREN WILSON • ROGER BARNARD

Published by
Pearson Longman Asia ELT
20/F Cornwall House
Taikoo Place
979 King's Road
Quarry Bay
Hong Kong

fax: +852 2856 9578
email: pearsonlongman.hk@pearson.com
www.pearsonlongman.com

and Associated Companies throughout the world.

First edition 1995
Second edition 1998
This edition 2007
Reprinted 2009

Produced by Pearson Education Asia Limited, Hong Kong
GCC/07

ISBN-13: 978-962-00-5666-6

Publisher: Rachel Wilson
Editor: Michael Tom
Designers: Junko Funaki, Annie Chan
Illustrators: Roger Barnard, Megan Cash, Andrew Lange, Teddy Wong

Acknowledgments

We would like to thank the following reviewers for the insightful feedback
provided for this edition: Yu-Ping Chang, Pei-Ling (Bessie) Chuang, Patrick
Davis, John Doodigian, William Figoni, Daniel Gossman, Jennifer Hickey,
Christopher Kerr, Kitai Kim, Carmella Lieske, Moon-Jeong Lim, John
Matthews, Michael S. Neiburg, Hugh Palmer, Trafford Parry, Caleb Prichard,
Andrew Reinmann, Richard H. Schaepe, Mike Shearer, Kenji Takahashi,
Marissa Troxell and David Whitmore.

CONTENTS

INTRODUCTION   vi

GETTING STARTED   Warm-up exercises   Glad to meet you.   2
Personal information   Listening task   So how do you know Jack, Maria?   3
                         Speaking task one   She lives in Yokohama.   4
                         Speaking task two   Is your hobby photography?   4

1 JUST ASKING   Warm-up exercises   I'd like some information about the trains.   5
Asking for information   Listening task   Could you tell me what time it's over?   6
                         Speaking task one   It leaves at ten o'clock.   7
                         Speaking task two   Could you tell me the best time of the year to
                                              visit Greece?   8
                         Homework   It finishes at 10:30.   9

2 IT'S BLACK AND WHITE   Warm-up exercises   What does it look like?   10
Describing things   Listening task   It's made of leather.   11
                         Speaking task one   It's small, and it has a handle.   12
                         Speaking task two   Is it big?   13
                         Homework   Does it have keys?   14

3 WOULD YOU MIND?   Warm-up exercises   Would you mind turning down the volume?   15
Making requests   Listening task   Sure, I'd be glad to.   16
                         Speaking task one   I'm afraid I can't.   17
                         Speaking task two   Could you possibly lend me ten dollars?   18
                         Homework   Can you answer the telephone?   20

4 TURN IT CLOCKWISE   Warm-up exercises   Could you tell me how to buy a ticket?   21
Giving instructions   Listening task   Could you tell me how to use these headphones?   22
                         Speaking task one   Place the paper face down on the glass.   23
                         Speaking task two   Laura, point at the window and push Michael.   25
                         Homework   Listen for instructions from crew.   26

5 SAY THAT AGAIN   Review exercises   Could you open the window for me?   27
Review and consolidation Listening task   Do you know if it has a hood?   28
                         Speaking task one   First, push the "power" button.   29
                         Speaking task two   Could I borrow your car tonight?   30
                         Language game   Put in the money and press this button.   31

6 GO RIGHT AHEAD   Warm-up exercises   Can I borrow some sugar?   32
Asking for permission   Listening task   Do you mind if I leave class early today?   33
                         Speaking task one   I'm sorry, but I have to use it this weekend.   34
                         Speaking task two   Sure, go ahead.   35
                         Homework   Mind if I smoke?   37

7 EXCUSES, EXCUSES   Warm-up exercises   Why didn't you call me?   38
Making excuses and   Listening task   I'm sorry, but I read the wrong chapter.   39
giving reasons   Speaking task one   I couldn't find the vacuum cleaner.   40
                         Speaking task two   Did you get a haircut yesterday?   41
                         Homework   I had to go to a wedding.   42

8 COULDN'T AGREE MORE
Giving opinions

Warm-up exercises   I think the city is great.   43
Listening task   In my opinion we should all stick together.   44
Speaking task one   I agree. It's wrong to ignore them.   45
Speaking task two   Keiko, what do you think about watching sports on TV?   47
Homework   I don't think teachers should give a lot of homework.   48

9 BIGGER AND BETTER
Comparing things

Warm-up exercises   Which do you like more, motorcycles or cars?   49
Listening task   He's much more handsome.   50
Speaking task one   Is your car more expensive than a BMW?   51
Speaking task two   The yard's cleaner today.   53
Homework   Do you think soccer is more exciting than baseball?   54

10 SAY THAT AGAIN
Review and consolidation

Review exercises   Do you mind if I call the electrician?   55
Listening task   But Mom, why can't I get a motorcycle?   56
Speaking task one   Mind if I open the door?   57
Speaking task two   I didn't exercise because I got up late.   59
Language game   What do you think of life in New York?   60

11 IF I WERE YOU
Giving advice and making suggestions

Warm-up exercises   What's the matter?   61
Listening task   Maybe you'd better rent one of those big party tents.   62
Speaking task one   What's wrong?   63
Speaking task two   I found a paper bag with $500 in it!   65
Homework   Why don't we go to a movie?   66

12 HAVE YOU EVER ... ?
Talking about experiences

Warm-up exercises   Have you ever been bungee jumping?   67
Listening task   Wow! Was anyone hurt?   68
Speaking task one   Has Nicole ever been on a boat?   69
Speaking task two   It happened when I was little.   71
Homework   Have you ever won a contest?   72

13 HOW ABOUT DINNER?
Inviting

Warm-up exercises   How about going to the beach tomorrow?   73
Listening task   Are you busy this weekend?   74
Speaking task one   Sure, I'd love to.   75
Speaking task two   I'm sorry, but I have to work.   76
Homework   Would you like to go to a movie Sunday night?   77

14 IT'S GONNA RAIN
Making predictions

Warm-up exercises   They're definitely going to win.   78
Listening task   But maybe he'll never come back!   79
Speaking task one   I think you'll be famous someday.   80
Speaking task two   Most people think space travel will be commonplace.   81
Homework   It will probably rain tomorrow.   82

15 SAY THAT AGAIN
Review and consolidation

Review exercises   Have you ever met a movie star?   83
Listening task   I think we'll be eaten alive by mosquitoes.   84
Speaking task one   What's 1 down?   85
Speaking task two   I think it's all a lie!   86
Language game   Can I close the door?   87

APPENDIX   89

STUDENT B PAGES   90

SELF-STUDY EXERCISES   103

SELF-STUDY EXERCISES ANSWER KEY   115

AUDIO SCRIPT   117

Acknowledgments

We would like to thank the teachers and students at the following schools for their valuable help in developing and revising this material:

- Athénée-Français, Tokyo
- Community English Program, Teachers College, Columbia University, New York
- Cosmopolitan Language Institute, Tokyo
- English Language Institute, Queens College, New York
- Haggerty English Language Program, SUNY New Paltz, New York
- International English Language Institute, Hunter College, New York
- Tama Art University, Tokyo
- Tokyo School of Business, Tokyo

We would also like to thank those at Prentice Hall who worked on this project originally, particularly our first production editor, Noël Vreeland Carter. For this new edition, we owe much to our publisher, Rachel Wilson, our editor, Michael Tom, our design manager, Winnie Sung, and her team of talented designers including Junko Funaki, Tonic Ng and Annie Chan, and all the great people at Pearson Longman.

For Masako, Sophie, In Sook, Mia and Dale.

R.B.
W.W.
Tokyo / New York
September 2006

INTRODUCTION

Fifty-Fifty Third Edition is a three-level course in communicative English that provides listening and speaking practice for students from the elementary level through the intermediate level. Designed primarily for use in large classes where "student talking" time is usually very limited, this material can be used effectively in virtually any size class since students actively participate in meaningful exchanges during pair work and group work. The focus is on listening and speaking proficiency. *Fifty-Fifty* Third Edition provides realistic yet manageable listening tasks, and extended pair work and group work tasks, all of which are designed to reduce learner anxiety and promote language acquisition via student participation in purposeful interaction.

Fifty-Fifty Book Two has been designed as a follow-up course to *Fifty-Fifty Book One* and can be used in classes at the intermediate level. The text consists of a warm-up unit, twelve main units and three review units. The *Appendix* contains the *Student B pages* of the pair work and group work activities, the *Self-study exercises* with answer key for out-of-class review and the *Audio script* for the listening tasks.

Each unit consists of the following sections. (The format of the review units differs slightly.)

● Warm-up exercises

Each unit begins with some simple warm-up exercises. *Exercise 1* is in the form of a comic sketch. The sketch has a question or an answer to be written by the student. The sketch illustrates the unit theme and introduces, in a simple context, the language to be practiced.

Exercise 2 and *Exercise 3* center on a dialogue that functions as a model that the students can listen to and practice reading through with a partner. The dialogue can also be used for freer conversation practice in which the students supply their own information.

● Listening task

The *Listening task* helps the students focus on the particular language points to be practiced. The students are not expected to retain or reproduce *all* the language they hear on the recording, but their aural comprehension of the target structures and vocabulary will increase as they listen for the information needed to complete the task.

It is suggested that the students listen several times: once to familiarize the students with the content, then again with pauses as the students complete the task and once more straight through as they check their answers. After the teacher has elicited the answers, the students could listen a final time, perhaps while going over the audio script. The *Audio script* for the *Listening task* is located in the *Appendix* and can also be used for extended practice and/or review of grammar and vocabulary. The *Teacher's Edition* provides helpful hints, as well as the answers, to ensure that the exercise goes smoothly.

● Speaking task one

Speaking task one provides communicative practice that maximizes "student talking" time. Students complete the task by asking partners for missing information. Being task-based, the exercise provides more than just question-and-answer practice: genuine communication takes place. The completion of each task relies on actual information sharing and feedback between students conversing in pairs.

It is suggested that the teacher try having students sit face to face, if possible, and maintain eye contact while speaking. They should avoid looking at each other's pages and should always ask for spelling or repetition in English. It is advisable to circulate once quickly at the outset to make sure that each student understands what to do and gets off to a good start. Correction techniques vary from teacher to teacher and exercise to exercise; however, during communicative practice it is usually advisable to leave most correction until afterward. The point of the tasks is communication, not the production of flawless sentences. (Nevertheless, errors that interfere with comprehension and/or are counterproductive to the practice should be rectified appropriately.)

Finally, the teacher can check the finished work by scanning students' pages and briefly querying their partners to verify answers. Students can also confer and compare answers themselves.

Speaking task two

Speaking task two is generally a bit "freer" than *Speaking task one* and is meant to provide additional practice in a slightly different context. *Speaking task two* exercises include "Find someone who" activities, group interviews and various types of language games that promote interaction while lessening learner anxiety.

All suggestions given above for *Speaking task one* apply to this section; the recommended procedures are the same.

Language game

In the review units, *Speaking task two* is followed by a section labeled *Language game*, an activity that encourages focused listening. The point of the game is to provide ample comprehensible input containing vocabulary and structures from the preceding units, as well as pronunciation practice—hopefully more in an atmosphere of fun, and less of conscious language study.

Homework

The last page of each main unit contains the *Homework* section, which is a brief writing assignment that students must do on a separate sheet of paper to be handed in. The *Homework* section includes a *Homework review* exercise, an optional follow-up exercise for in-class use, time permitting. Please note that some of these exercises might require the teacher's correction of the students' written homework before it is used as an oral/aural activity in class.

Language focus

The *Language focus* section at the end of each main unit contains an overview of the sentence structures presented in the unit, providing language models for the students that they can use for a quick reference while doing the exercises.

Student B pages

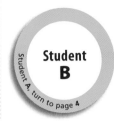

Student A, turn to page 4

This section in the *Appendix* contains all the pages necessary for the information gap activities, when students working in pairs or small groups must look at different pages. In the units, these activities contain a page reference in the upper right-hand corner. It might be a good idea to remind students not to look at their partner's pages or to flip back and forth between the *Student A* and *Student B pages*.

Self-study exercises and Answer key

The *Self-study exercises* in the *Appendix* review and consolidate material covered in the twelve main units, providing students with added listening practice through recycling some of the *Listening task* audio. The accompanying *Answer key* provides all of the answers to the *Self-study exercises* and enables students to assess their own performance and their progress towards aural mastery of the listening material. Students can download the *Self-study Audio* by visiting the *Fifty-Fifty* website at www.fifty-fifty-series.com

Audio script

The *Audio script* in the *Appendix* contains the *Listening task* material. The introductory dialogue in the *Warm-up exercises* of each unit is not included in the *Audio script* since the dialogue itself serves as the script.

In addition to the Student Book, the Fifty-Fifty series includes the following components:
* Teacher's Edition with Test Master CD-ROM Pack
* Class CD
* Companion Website: www.fifty-fifty-series.com
* Downloadable: Self-study Audio
* Downloadable: Class Audio

The authors hope you and your students enjoy using *Fifty-Fifty* Third Edition and would appreciate any comments or suggestions you might have. They can be contacted via the *Fifty-Fifty* website.

GETTING STARTED

Personal information

Warm-up exercises

Exercise 1

Write a reply.

Exercise 2 1

Listen to the following conversation. Then practice it with a partner.

> **Memo**
> Always look at the person you are
> speaking to. Don't look down at the page!

Paul	Hello. I'm Paul Savage.
Jane	Nice to meet you. My name's Jane … Jane Chung.
Paul	Glad to meet you, Jane. Where are you from?
Jane	Well, I'm from San Francisco, but I live in New Jersey now. So, what do you do, Paul?
Paul	I'm studying Law here at Columbia. How about you?
Jane	I'm a software designer. I work for Nintendo.

Exercise 3

Practice the conversation a few more times. Each time, answer the questions with *true* information.

Listening task   Do Exercise 1 alone and Exercise 2 with a partner.

Exercise 1 2

Listen to the conversation and check (✓) all the correct information for John and Maria.

	is from L.A.	is from Denver	is from Chicago	lives in Denver	lives in Chicago	is a teacher	is a graphic designer	plays tennis	goes to art shows
John	☐	☐	☐	☐	☐	☐	☐	☐	☐
Maria	☐	☐	☐	☐	☐	☐	☐	☐	☐

Exercise 2

Work with a partner and take turns asking each other yes/no questions about John and Maria. (Ask questions with your book open and answer with your *book closed*.)

Example

Student A	Is Maria from Denver?	**Student A**	Does John live in Chicago?
Student B	No, she isn't.	**Student B**	Yes, he does.

Speaking task one

Exercise 1

Ask Student B questions about the people below and fill in the information in the boxes (1–3).

Student B, turn to page 90

Example			
Student A	Where does Jenny live?	**Student A**	What does she do?
Student B	She lives in Yokohama.	**Student B**	She's a waitress.

1 Personal information: Jenny Chang

Lives in: ....
Occupation: ....
Languages: ....
Hobbies: ....

2 Personal information: Carlos Lopez

Lives in: ....
Occupation: ....
Languages: ....
Hobbies: ....

3 Personal information: Ken and Pat Lee

Live in: ....
Occupations: ....
Languages: ....
Hobbies: ....

4 Personal information: Student B

Lives in: ....
Occupation: ....
Languages: ....
Hobbies: ....

Exercise 2

Ask Student B questions and fill in the information about Student B in box 4.

Speaking task two   Do this exercise with everyone.

Write where your partner (from *Speaking task one*, box 4) lives and your partner's hobbies on the board.

Walk around the classroom and talk to your classmates. Ask yes/no questions using the places and hobbies on the board. Find out where three of your classmates live and what their hobbies are, and fill in the boxes below.

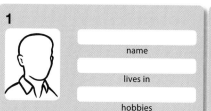

1
name
lives in
hobbies

2
name
lives in
hobbies

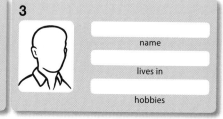

3
name
lives in
hobbies

1 JUST ASKING

Asking for information

Warm-up exercises

Exercise 1

Write a question for each answer.

Exercise 2 ◎ 3

Listen to the following conversation. Then practice it with a partner.

> **Memo**
>
> Always look at the person you are speaking to. Don't look down at the page!

Customer	I'd like some information about the trains.
Clerk	Yes?
Customer	Could you tell me what time the train to Miami leaves?
Clerk	Yes, the next train leaves at 11:00 a.m.
Customer	Do you know how long it takes?
Clerk	Let me see … It takes twenty-eight hours.

Exercise 3

Practice the conversation a few more times. Each time, ask and answer questions about a different city and times.

> **Memo**
>
> You are talking about trains from New York.

Seattle 65 hrs.
Boston 4 hrs.
New York
Chicago 19 hrs.
San Francisco 72 hrs.
Denver 19 hrs.
Dallas 22 hrs.
Miami 28 hrs.

Look at page 9
Language focus

5

Listening task

Exercise 1 4–7

Listen to the conversations (1–4) and write the number of each conversation next to the correct picture.

Exercise 2 4–7

Listen to the conversations again. For each of the questions, choose the best answer below and number them 1 to 8.

- Definitely. Call before you come.
- It shouldn't take more than 30 minutes.
- Let me see ... It's over at exactly 11:18.
- Parts were about 150, and the labor was 250.
- No, you can do that when you pick it up.
- No, not for about 2 hours.
- No, it won't be crowded tonight. Don't worry.
- It'll take about a week or two.

Exercise 3

Work in a small group and try to recall the questions for the answers.

Speaking task one

Exercise 1

You want to travel from New York to Chicago, but you do not know the best way to go. Note the time of day you would like to leave and then speak to Student B, a travel agent. Ask Student B for information about a bus and a flight. Write the answers below.

Memo

Change roles as Student A and Student B, and do the exercises again.

Example

Student B	Can I help you?
Student A	Yes, I'd like to go to Chicago.
Student B	How would you like to travel?
Student A	I'm not sure. I'd like some information on the buses and flights.
Student B	OK, I can help you.
Student A	Great! Could you tell me … ?

Bus

I'd like to leave around _____ o'clock.

How much?

Time leaves?

Time arrives?

How long?

Bus number?

Flight

I'd like to leave around _____ o'clock.

How much?

Time leaves?

Time arrives?

How long?

Flight number?

Exercise 2

You want to take a language course this summer. Student B is a language school manager. Choose a language to study and ask Student B for information. Make a note of your questions and the answers. (See the box below for ideas.)

Example

Student A	Could you tell me if you have a Chinese language course?
Student B	Yes, we do.
Student A	OK, could you tell me … ?

THINGS TO ASK ABOUT

- _____ language
- placement test
- teachers
- course dates
- length of course
- costs
- class times
- students
- school location

7

Group B, turn to page 92

Speaking task two Do this exercise with everyone.

The teacher will divide the class into two halves, Group A and Group B, and give each student in Group A one of the boxes below. Walk around the classroom and ask students in Group B for the information to write in your box.

Example		
Student A	Do you know how long it takes to go from England to France by ferry?	**Student A** Could you tell me the best month to travel through Australia?
Student B	Yes, it takes one and a half hours.	**Student B** I'm sorry, I don't know.

Memo
- Do not show your box to anyone!
- Group B students may stay in their seats.

1 Find someone who knows this information:
- It takes _____ to go from England to France by ferry.
- It costs _____ to go from England to France by ferry.
- _____ is the best season to visit Greece.

2 Find someone who knows this information:
- It costs _____ to take a horse-and-buggy ride in Central Park in New York City.
- _____ is the cheapest way to travel from New York to California.
- _____ are good places to go sightseeing in San Francisco.

3 Find someone who knows this information:
- It takes _____ to travel by train from Tokyo to Osaka.
- It costs _____ to travel by train from Tokyo to Osaka.
- Most of the subways stop running in Tokyo at about _____ o'clock.

4 Find someone who knows this information:
- _____ is the best month to travel through Australia.
- In July, the weather in Australia is _____.
- It takes _____ to fly from Australia to New Zealand.

5 Find someone who knows this information:
- In August, the weather in India is _____.
- In January, the weather in Thailand is _____.
- The banks open at _____ in the morning in Hong Kong.

6 Find someone who knows this information:
- It takes _____ to fly from New York to London.
- It costs _____ to fly from New York to London.
- It costs _____ to see a movie in London.

7 Find someone who knows this information:
- _____ is the best way to travel from Hong Kong to Macau.
- _____ are good places to go sightseeing in Beijing, China.
- _____ is the best season to trek in the Himalayas.

8 Find someone who knows this information:
- A cup of coffee costs _____ at a sidewalk café in Paris.
- The shops are closed from _____ to _____ for *siesta* in Barcelona, Spain.
- _____ are good places to go sightseeing in Athens, Greece.

Homework

Write a question and a full answer for each of the locations (1–6).

1

train station

2

classroom

3

hotel reception

4

airplane

5

movie theater

6

bank

Homework review

The teacher will have each student write one answer on the board. Then the class will try to guess the location and the question for each answer.

Example

(written on board)
- It finishes at 10:30.
- No, we don't have a quiz today.

Language focus

| I'd like some information about | the buses. the guided tours. | → | Sure. How can I help you? Yes? |

| Do you know Could you tell me | what time it finishes? how much it is? how long it takes? if you have a French course? the best time to arrive? | → | It finishes at 10:15. It's $14. Yes, it takes an hour and a half. Yes, we do. The best time to arrive is before 8:00 a.m. |

2 IT'S BLACK AND WHITE

Describing things

Warm-up exercises

Exercise 1

Write the man's answer.

Exercise 2   8

Listen to the following conversation. Then practice it with a partner.

Memo

Always look at the person you are speaking to. Don't look down at the page!

Customer	Excuse me, I left my briefcase under this table about an hour ago.
Waitress	What does it look like?
Customer	It's brown, and it has a black handle.
Waitress	Oh, yes. Does it have a combination lock?
Customer	Yes, it does.
Waitress	Right, the busboy found it. Wait here, I'll get it.

Exercise 3

Practice the conversation a few more times. Each time, ask and answer questions about a different bag.

Look at page 14
Language foc

Listening task

Exercise 1

Look at each sentence below (a–o) and write the letter below each object that it describes.

a It's made of leather.
b It has a handle.
c It's black.
d It has buttons.
e It's made mostly of plastic.

f It has a screen.
g It's brown.
h It's plain, with almost no design.
i It has batteries.
j It has switches.

k It has a strap.
l There are numbers on it.
m It has a lock.
n It's made of wood.
o It's square.

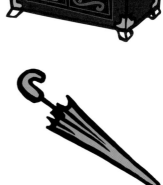

Exercise 2 9–14

Listen to the conversations (1–6) and write the number of each conversation above the correct object.

Exercise 3 9–14

Listen again and write the *keywords* next to each object.

Speaking task one   Do this exercise with a partner.

Student A

Choose six of the objects in the picture below, but do not tell Student B the names of the objects. Then describe each object to Student B until Student B correctly guesses the name of the object.

Student B

Listen to Student A describe six objects below and guess what each object is. Before you guess, ask questions to check!

Example

Student A	It's small, and it's made of glass and plastic. It has a handle.	Student B	Is it flat?
		Student A	Yes, it is.
		Student B	Is it the hand mirror?

Vocabulary

- teacup
- travel alarm
- hand mirror
- pitcher
- coffee mug
- watering can
- television
- birdcage
- golf clubs
- backpack
- poster
- CD player
- wall mirror
- toaster oven
- clock radio
- aquarium
- electric heater
- folding chair
- sports bag
- armchair

Memo

- Student A: don't say where each object is or what it is used for.
- Change roles as Student A and Student B, and do the exercise again.

Speaking task two
Do this exercise in a group of three or four students.

Student A
Choose one object in the room below, but do not say which object it is. Students B, C and D will ask you questions to find out which object it is. Answer all questions with "yes" or "no."

Students B, C and D
Take turns asking Student A yes/no questions. Try to guess Student A's object. Whoever guesses the object first wins, but if no one can guess it, Student A wins! The group can ask *twenty* questions, and each student can make no more than *three* guesses.

Memo
- Do *not* ask or say where an object is or what it is used for.
- Do this exercise several times. Each student take a turn as Student A.

Example

Student B	Does it have a handle?
Student A	No, it doesn't.
Student C	Is it made of wood?
Student A	Yes, it is.

Student D	Is it flat?
Student A	Yes, it is.
Student D	Is it the cutting board?

Vocabulary

- trash can
- frying pan
- pot
- tea kettle
- blender
- strainer
- colander
- dish
- scale
- bread knife
- cutting board
- sugar bowl
- teapot
- hourglass
- oven mitt

Homework

Find a large picture of an interesting object in a magazine or newspaper. Write a description of the object. (Write three or more sentences.) Cut out the picture and bring it to class.

Example

- It's small and square.
- It's mostly made of plastic.
- It has keys and a screen.

Homework review   Work in a group of three or four students.

The teacher will put everyone's picture on the board and number each picture.

Student A
Choose *any* picture on the board. (It does *not* have to be your picture.) Answer questions ("yes" or "no") until someone guesses the picture.

Students B, C and D
Take turns asking Student A yes/no questions about the objects on the board until you can guess the correct picture.

Example

Student B	Is it made of plastic?
Student A	Yes, it is.
Student C	Does it have a handle?
Student A	No, it doesn't.
Student D	Does it have keys?
Student A	Yes, it does.
Student D	Is it picture number five?
Student A	Yes!

Language focus

What does it look like?
Could you tell me what it looks like?
Do you know what it looks like?

It's	small long	and	square. flat.
	black, dark blue,	and it has	stripes. a handle.
It has	a zipper. buttons.		

What is it made of?
Could you tell me what it's made of?
Do you know what it's made of?

It's made of
It's partly made of
It's mostly made of
leather. wood. cotton. metal.

3 WOULD YOU MIND?

Making requests

Warm-up exercises

Look at page 20

Exercise 1

Write the woman's answer.

Do you think you could give me a push?

Exercise 2 15

Listen to the following conversation. Then practice it with a partner.

Memo

Always look at the person you are speaking to. Don't look down at the page!

Mom	Joey, would you mind turning down the volume?
Joey	Not at all.
Mom	Could you possibly clean your room this afternoon?
Joey	Sorry, but I have to go to soccer practice.
Mom	Well, do you think you could do it after dinner?
Joey	Sure, no problem.

Exercise 3

Practice the conversation a few more times. Each time, ask and answer about a different request. Use an idea below or your own idea.

Listening task

Exercise 1 16

Listen to the conversation and circle the things that Julie asks Alex to do.

Exercise 2 16

Listen again and check (✓) all the things that Alex agrees to do and make an "✗" on the things he cannot do.

Exercise 3 16

Listen once more and make a note of *why* he cannot do some things.

Speaking task one   Do these exercises with a partner.

Exercise 1

Make an "✗" on six of the things below that you do *not* want to do for your partner and think of a reason to say "no." (Do not show your partner which six things you have chosen.)

Memo

First discuss the possible requests for each picture, as well as possible reasons to refuse requests.

Exercise 2

Take turns with your partner asking each other to do things:

- Choose any picture—marked or unmarked—and ask your partner to do something.
- When your partner asks you to do something, say "no" to anything marked with an "✗" and say "yes" to anything not marked.

The first person to get his or her partner to say "yes" to six things wins!

Memo

Always give a *different reason* when you say "no."

Example

| **Student A** | Do you think you could feed the cat? | **Student B** | Could you possibly pick me up later? |
| **Student B** | Sure, I'd be glad to. | **Student A** | I'm afraid I can't. I have to go to the library. |

Speaking task two   Do this exercise with everyone.

The teacher will give you *one* of the boxes (1–8) on pages 18 and 19. Walk around the classroom and ask your classmates to do things for you, and agree or refuse to do things for others.

Ask your classmates to do things and write the name of someone who says "yes." ➡

Use this information to answer requests. (Say "yes" to these three things only.) ➡

Memo
- Use only page 18 if there are fewer than eight students in the class.
- Do not show your box to anyone!
- Talk in *pairs*, not groups.

---

1 Find someone who:

ASK

_____ name _____ will drive you to the airport tomorrow evening.

_____ name _____ will babysit your little brother tonight.

_____ name _____ will let you copy yesterday's class notes.

ANSWER

Agree to:
- pick up some books at the library.
- lend your friend ten dollars.
- take care of your friend's cat this summer.

Refuse all other requests!

---

2 Find someone who:

ASK

_____ name _____ will lend you ten dollars.

_____ name _____ will help you look for your dog.

_____ name _____ will water your houseplants while you are away next week.

ANSWER

Agree to:
- let your friend copy your class notes.
- help your friend carry some boxes downstairs.
- go to the post office for your friend.

Refuse all other requests!

---

3 Find someone who:

ASK

_____ name _____ will help you with the homework after school.

_____ name _____ will take care of your cat for a month this summer.

_____ name _____ will go to the post office and mail some letters for you.

ANSWER

Agree to:
- teach your friend how to use the computer lab.
- water your friend's houseplants.
- babysit your friend's little brother.

Refuse all other requests!

---

4 Find someone who:

ASK

_____ name _____ will teach you how to use the computer lab after class.

_____ name _____ will pick up some books for you at the library this afternoon.

_____ name _____ will help you carry some boxes downstairs.

ANSWER

Agree to:
- drive your friend to the airport.
- look for your friend's dog.
- help your friend with the homework.

Refuse all other requests!

Example

Student A	Do you think you could help me look for my dog?
Student B	Of course.

Student C	Could you possibly help me paint my kitchen this afternoon?
Student D	I'm sorry, but I have a dentist appointment.

Memo

- Always give a *reason* when you refuse a request.
- "Your friend" means the person you are speaking to.

---

5 Find someone who:

ASK

- [name] will lend you a dictionary.
- [name] will pick up your laundry tomorrow morning.
- [name] will help you paint your kitchen this afternoon.

ANSWER

Agree to:
- lend your friend a camcorder.
- let your friend copy your homework.
- show your friend how to install new computer software.

Refuse all other requests!

---

6 Find someone who:

ASK

- [name] will let you copy the homework for tomorrow.
- [name] will help you move to a new house on Sunday.
- [name] will feed your goldfish while you are on vacation next week.

ANSWER

Agree to:
- lend your friend a dictionary.
- go to the bank for your friend.
- go to the supermarket for your friend.

Refuse all other requests!

---

7 Find someone who:

ASK

- [name] will help you fix your car.
- [name] will show you how to install new computer software.
- [name] will go to the supermarket for you.

ANSWER

Agree to:
- explain the class project to your friend.
- feed your friend's goldfish.
- pick up your friend's laundry.

Refuse all other requests!

---

8 Find someone who:

ASK

- [name] will explain the class project to you after school.
- [name] will lend you a camcorder for a week.
- [name] will go to the bank for you this afternoon.

ANSWER

Agree to:
- help paint your friend's kitchen.
- help your friend move to a new house.
- help fix your friend's car.

Refuse all other requests!

Homework

Match the dialogues with the pictures and write the request for each dialogue.

1 **Stella** [Makes a request.]
Lisa I'm in the kitchen, and my hands are full right now, Stella. Can you get it?
Stella Oh, all right, but it's probably for you.

2 **Professor Hall** Yes, Ann-Marie, what is it?
Ann-Marie [Makes a request.]
Professor Hall Of course. I'll be in my office after 3:00.
Ann-Marie Great, thank you. I'll come at 3:30.

3 **Jack** I'm going to the store, Jill. Need anything?
Jill [Makes a request.]
Jack What kind do you want?
Jill Oh, it doesn't matter. Just get a large one.

4 **Mom** [Makes a request.]
Tommy But I just walked him an hour ago!
Mom That was more like *three* hours ago, and anyway, he wants to go out.
Tommy Oh, OK. Here, boy! Let's go.

   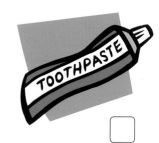

Homework review Do this exercise with everyone.

Walk around and talk to your classmates. Read through the dialogues. For each dialogue, find someone who wrote a request *similar* to yours and write that person's name next to your request.

Language focus

		Yes	No	
Can you / Could you	close the door? / lend me your pen?	Sure.		
Do you think you could / Could you possibly	meet me after school? / pick me up tomorrow?	Of course. / I'd be glad to.	I'm sorry, but I wish I could, but I'd like to, but I'm afraid I can't.	I'm very busy. I have to work
Would it be possible for you to / I was wondering if you could possibly	help me move tomorrow? / take me to the airport later?	No problem.		
Would you mind	closing the door? / turning down the volume?	Not at all. / No, not at all.		

4 TURN IT CLOCKWISE
Giving instructions

Warm-up exercises

Exercise 1

Write the second man's question.

Any questions?

Trainee

Exercise 2 🔘 17

Listen to the following conversation. Then practice it with a partner.

Memo
Always look at the person you are speaking to. Don't look down at the page!

Man	Excuse me, could you tell me how to buy a ticket?
Woman	Sure. First, find your station and the fare on the map.
Man	OK, I got it. It's West Park, $2.50.
Woman	Then, put in the money.
Man	Right, OK.
Woman	After that, push the button for "$2.50" and take your ticket and change.

Exercise 3

Practice the conversation a few more times. Each time, choose a different station from the map below.

Memo
You are at *Lakeview* station.

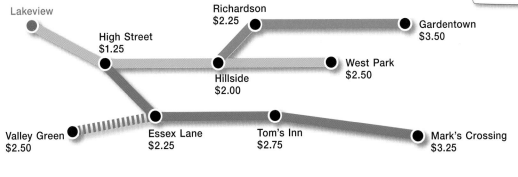

Lakeview

Richardson $2.25

High Street $1.25

Gardentown $3.50

Hillside $2.00

West Park $2.50

Valley Green $2.50

Essex Lane $2.25

Tom's Inn $2.75

Mark's Crossing $3.25

Look at page 26

Language focus

Listening task

Listen to six conversations between a flight attendant and two passengers (a husband and wife). Write the number of each conversation next to the correct picture (1–6).

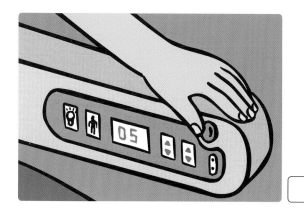

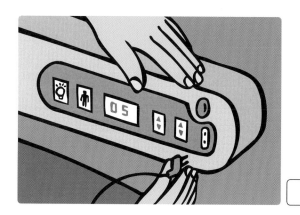

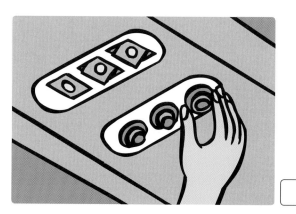

Now listen to six *different* conversations between the husband and wife. On each of the pictures (1–6), write "H" if the husband is right or "W" if the wife is right.

Speaking task one
Do Exercise 1 with a partner and Exercise 2 with everyone.

Exercise 1

The teacher will give each pair of students a set of six pictures (set A, B, C or D) from page 23 or 24. Each pair should work together and write down instructions for their pictures, that is, how to use the machine.

A Copy machine

Vocabulary

- lid/cover
- face down
- glass
- select
- push/press
- "start" button

B Photo booth

Vocabulary

- adjust
- curtain
- select
- photo size
- insert / put in
- tray

C Gasoline pump

Vocabulary

- nozzle
- gas pump
- lever
- insert / put in
- gas tank
- replace

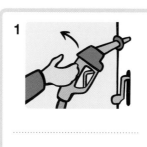  

1 .... 2 .... 3 ....

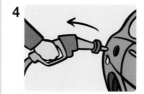  

4 .... 5 .... 6 ....

D Coin laundry machine

Vocabulary

- laundry
- pour
- detergent
- compartment
- select/set
- insert / put in

1 .... 2 .... 3 ....

4 WASH TEMP.
warm cold
hot

5 .... 6 ....

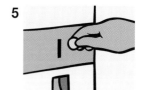 

Exercise 2

For each of the *other* three sets of pictures, walk around the classroom and find someone to give you the instructions and write them below the pictures.

Example

| Student A | Excuse me. Could you tell me how to use the photo booth? |
| Student B | Sure. First, you adjust the seat. Then, you … |

Speaking task two   Do each exercise in different groups.

Exercise 1

In groups of three, take turns doing the actions in the box. Then, as a group, think of six more actions and add them to the list.

Vocabulary

ACTIONS

- crawl
- cry
- frown at
- grab
- hug
- jump
- kick
- kneel
- laugh at
- lean on
- open
- pick up

- pinch
- point at
- pound on
- pull
- punch
- push
- scratch
- scream at
- shake
- skip
- slap
- smile at

- squeeze
- throw
- tickle
- turn around
- wave to
- wink at

Exercise 2

Form *new* groups of three and write a *silent movie scene* for two people—Student A and Student B—who will each act out six or more actions during the scene. (Use actions in the box above.)

Example

(Make three copies of the scene, one for each student.)
Student A, point at the window and push Student B.
Student B, go to the window and wink at Student A.
Student A, go and stand behind Student B, turn around and cry.

Exercise 3

Again, form new groups of three. Take turns as the *director* of the movie scene that you wrote in Exercise 2 and give instructions to the two *actors/actresses*—Student A and Student B. (Use their names in the instructions.)

Example

Director	Laura, point at the window and push Michael.
Laura	[Points at the window and pushes Michael.]
Director	Good. Now, Michael, go to the window and wink at Laura.
Michael	[Goes to the window and winks at Laura.]
Director	OK. Laura, go and stand behind Michael, turn around and cry.

Homework

Write instructions for each *subway sign* (1–6).

Example

Listen for instructions from crew.

Memo

Write the instructions on a separate sheet of paper.

Vocabulary

- hand straps
- cars
- lean
- emergency brake

1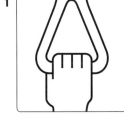

2

3

4

5

6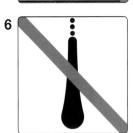

Homework review   Do this exercise with everyone.

Walk around and talk to your classmates. Compare your instructions for the signs (1–6). For each one, find someone who wrote instructions *similar* to yours and write that person's name next to your instructions.

Memo

- Do this exercise in the next lesson if you have time.
- If you cannot find anyone, write "no one."

Language focus

How can I
How do you
Could you tell me how to

buy a parking receipt from this machine?

First, put in the money for the amount of time you want.
Then, push this green button.
After that, take your receipt from the machine.

Review exercises   Do these exercises with a partner.

Exercise 1

The teacher will give you one of the pictures (1–4) below. Each picture has the first line of a dialogue. Write two or more additional lines of dialogue for the picture.

1

Man Could I have some information about the bungee jumping?

2

Man Your bag? What does it look like?

3

Boy Mrs. Jones, could you open the window for me?

4

Wife Honey? I'm glad you're home. Could you tell me again how to turn off the new oven?

Exercise 2

Say your lines to the class (with your partner). Do *not* say the first line of the dialogue above. The class will guess your picture.

Listening task

Exercise 1 30–34

Listen to the conversations (1–5) with your *book closed*. Then open your book and write the number of each conversation next to the correct picture.

Exercise 2 30–34

Listen again and write the *keywords* next to each picture.

Memo

Keywords are important words that tell you which picture to choose.

28

Speaking task one Do this exercise with a partner.

Student A

Choose six of the objects in the room below, but do not tell Student B the names of the objects. Then describe each object to Student B and tell Student B how to use it. Answer Student B's questions until Student B correctly guesses the object.

Student B

Listen to Student A describe six objects below and how to use them. Guess what each object is. Before you guess, ask questions to check!

Example

Student A	They're small and made of metal. First, you pick them up. Then, you move them up and down.	Student B	Are they black?
		Student A	Yes, they are.
		Student B	Are they weights?

Speaking task two   Do Exercise 1 alone and Exercise 2 with everyone.

Exercise 1

The teacher will divide the class into two halves, Group A and Group B.

Group A
Mark six things below that you need to borrow from your classmates.

Group B
Mark four things below that you will lend to four of your classmates.

Exercise 2

Group A students will walk around the classroom and Group B students will stay in their seats.

Group A
Try to borrow each thing you marked above from one of your classmates in Group B. (Try to borrow each thing from a different classmate.)

Group B
Lend each thing you marked to the first person who asks you. You can only lend each thing *one* time. Refuse to lend the unmarked things and *give a reason*.

> **Memo**
> - Do not look at anyone's page.
> - Change groups and do the exercise again.

Example

Student A	Could you possibly lend me your bicycle this afternoon?
Student B	Sure, no problem.

Student A	Do you think you could lend me your tennis racket?
Student B	I'm sorry, but my sister's using it.

⑤

Language game Play this game with two to four "players" and one "caller."

Take turns choosing two numbers (1–24) from the grid below. Each number is a question or an answer. The caller will read each sentence that you choose.

Choose one number, listen to the caller read the sentence and then choose another number. Try to match a question with the answer. Do not write any notes. Just listen!

Continue until all the questions and answers have been matched. The player with the most matches wins!

Caller, turn to page 93

> **Memo**
> - Cross off (✗) all matched numbers and circle *your* matches.
> - Look at this page only!
> - The teacher may let you write notes on the numbers.

Example

Player A	Number 4.	**Player B**	Number 23.
Caller	"Could you lend me your pen?"	**Caller**	"Of course. Here you are."
Player A	Number 11.	**Player B**	Number 4.
Caller	"Is it big?" They don't match!	**Caller**	"Could you lend me your pen?" They match!

1 2 3 4 5 6

7 8 9 10 11 12

13 14 15 16 17 18

19 20 21 22 23 24

6 Go Right Ahead
Asking for permission

Warm-up exercises

Exercise 1

Write the woman's question.

?

I'm sorry, but I have to use it.

Exercise 2 35

Listen to the following conversation. Then practice it with a partner.

> **Memo**
>
> Always look at the person you are speaking to. Don't look down at the page!

Alice	Hi, Mary! Can I borrow some sugar?
Mary	Of course. Come on in.
Alice	Could I also borrow your large mixing bowl?
Mary	Well, sure. Do you need anything else?
Alice	Would it be possible for me to use your oven?
Mary	My oven? Sorry, I'm afraid I have to use it today.

Exercise 3

Practice the conversation a few more times. Each time, ask to borrow different things.

Look at page 37
Language fo...

Listening task

Exercise 1 36–45

Before you listen to the conversations, guess what the request for permission will be for each picture. Listen to each conversation and see if you were correct.

1  2  3  4 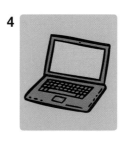 5

6  7  8  9  10

Exercise 2 36–45

Listen to each conversation again. For each one (1–10), make a check (✓) in the box for "Permission given" or "Permission refused."

	Permission given	Permission refused	Reply:
1	☐	☐	
2	☐	☐	
3	☐	☐	
4	☐	☐	
5	☐	☐	
6	☐	☐	
7	☐	☐	
8	☐	☐	
9	☐	☐	
10	☐	☐	

Exercise 3 36–45

Listen to each conversation once more. Make a note of the *reply* in each one (1–10).

> **Memo**
> In Exercise 3, you can write a short sentence or just a few words.

Student B, turn to page 94

Student A

Speaking task one

Exercise 1

You are a college student. Student B is your roommate. Ask Student B if you can:

Check (✓): Permission given refused

- wear Student B's new sweater on a date.
- watch a movie on TV tonight.
- use Student B's computer to do some homework.
- have a small party next Saturday night.
- use Student B's camera this weekend.
- invite a few friends over to play cards.
- borrow Student B's car Friday night.
- take Student B's CD player to the beach.

Example

Student A Is it OK if I wear your new sweater on a date?

Student B Sure, go ahead.

Exercise 2

You are Student B's boss. Student B is an office worker. Look at the information below. Answer Student B's requests. (You can give *or* refuse permission.)

Student B is a very good worker. You usually say "yes" to Student B's requests, but remember these things:

- The company car can only be used for business.
- There is an important company meeting early Monday morning.
- This summer you want all the workers to take short vacations.

Exercise 3

You are a student. Student B is your teacher. Ask Student B for permission to:

Check (✓): Permission given refused

- borrow Student B's dictionary.
- leave class early today.
- hand in the book report one day late.
- come to class late tomorrow.
- change the subject of your History report.
- go to the restroom.
- take a make-up test for the exam you missed.
- miss class on Monday.

Exercise 4

You are Student B's parent. Student B is a teenager. Look at the information below. Answer Student B's requests. (You can give *or* refuse permission.)

Student B is a good son/daughter. You usually say "yes" to Student B's requests, but remember these things:

- Student B has to study more after school and in the evening.
- You hate motorcycles. They are too dangerous.
- Student B is too young to go on a trip overseas with friends.

Speaking task two   Do this exercise with everyone.

The teacher will give you *one* of the boxes (1–8) on pages 35 and 36. Walk around and talk to your classmates.

> Ask your classmates for permission and write the name of someone who says "yes."

➡️

> Use this information to answer requests. (Say "yes" to these three things only.)

➡️

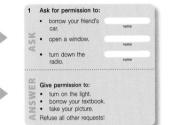

Memo

- Use only page 35 if there are fewer than eight students in the class.
- Do not show your box to anyone!
- Talk in *pairs*, not groups.

---

1   Ask for permission to:

ASK

- borrow your friend's car.   _____ name
- open a window.   _____ name
- turn down the radio.   _____ name

ANSWER

Give permission to:
- turn on the light.
- borrow your textbook.
- take your picture.

Refuse all other requests!

---

2   Ask for permission to:

ASK

- use your friend's computer.   _____ name
- close the door.   _____ name
- borrow your friend's textbook.   _____ name

ANSWER

Give permission to:
- turn down the radio.
- use your telephone.
- borrow your sweater.

Refuse all other requests!

---

3   Ask for permission to:

ASK

- take your friend's picture.   _____ name
- borrow your friend's sweater.   _____ name
- turn off the TV.   _____ name

ANSWER

Give permission to:
- use your computer.
- open a window.
- borrow your bicycle.

Refuse all other requests!

---

4   Ask for permission to:

ASK

- borrow your friend's bicycle.   _____ name
- turn on the light.   _____ name
- use your friend's telephone.   _____ name

ANSWER

Give permission to:
- borrow your car.
- close the door.
- turn off the TV.

Refuse all other requests!

Example

| Student A | Would it be possible for me to borrow your car? |
| Student B | Sure. |

| Student C | OK if I close a window? |
| Student D | Well, I'd rather you didn't. It's hot in here. |

Memo

- Always give a *reason* when you refuse a request.
- "Your friend" means the person you are speaking to.

5 **Ask for permission to:**

ASK

- use your friend's cell phone.   name
- close a window.   name
- turn on the TV.   name

ANSWER

Give permission to:
- play with your dog.
- borrow your skis.
- watch a movie on TV.

Refuse all other requests!

6 **Ask for permission to:**

ASK

- turn up the heat.   name
- read your friend's diary.   name
- borrow your friend's skis.   name

ANSWER

Give permission to:
- turn on the TV.
- use your motorcycle.
- turn off the light.

Refuse all other requests!

7 **Ask for permission to:**

ASK

- watch a movie on TV.   name
- turn off the light.   name
- borrow your friend's fishing pole.   name

ANSWER

Give permission to:
- turn up the heat.
- close a window.
- open the door.

Refuse all other requests!

8 **Ask for permission to:**

ASK

- open the door.   name
- play with your friend's dog.   name
- use your friend's motorcycle.   name

ANSWER

Give permission to:
- use your cell phone.
- read your diary.
- borrow your fishing pole.

Refuse all other requests!

Homework

Match the dialogues with the pictures and write a request for permission for each dialogue.

1 **Rob**   [Requests permission.]
    Amber No, go right ahead, Rob.
    Rob   Thanks. I'll open a window so it won't bother you.
    Amber No, that's OK. Don't worry about it.

2 **Tommy** [Requests permission.]
    Dad   Where to, Tommy?
    Tommy To my pen pal in Japan. I want to say, "Happy birthday."
    Dad   Well, OK, but don't talk too long.

3 **Rene**   [Requests permission.]
    Ali   Sure, Rene. You can use it all day.
    Rene   Thanks, but I just need it for a minute. I have one in my locker.
    Ali   Oh, OK.

4 **Eric**   [Requests permission.]
    Josh   Sunday? Where do you want to go?
    Eric   I'd like to take Rebecca for a ride in the mountains.
    Josh   OK, but be careful, Eric.

 ☐    ☐    ☐    ☐

Homework review Do this exercise with everyone.

Walk around and talk to your classmates. Read through the dialogues. For each dialogue, find someone who wrote a request for permission *similar* to yours and write that person's name next to your request.

Language focus

		Yes	No	
OK if I	sit down?		I'm afraid not.	
Can I	close the door?		I'd rather you didn't.	
Could I	borrow your pen?	Sure.		
Is it OK if I / Is it all right if I	use your phone? / wear your jacket?	Sure, go ahead. / Of course.		
I wonder if I could / Would it be possible for me to	borrow your camera? / use your car?		I'm sorry, but / Sorry, but I'm afraid that	it doesn't work. / I have to use it.
Mind if I / Do you mind if I	borrow your bicycle? / use your phone?	Not at all. / No, go ahead. / No, please do.		

7 EXCUSES, EXCUSES
Making excuses and giving reasons

Warm-up exercises

Exercise 1

Write the boy's answer.

Exercise 2 46

Listen to the following conversation. Then practice it with a partner.

Ann	Where were you? I waited for two hours last night!
Patrick	I'm sorry, Ann, but I had to drive to the airport.
Ann	Why didn't you call me?
Patrick	Oh, well, I couldn't find your office number.
Ann	Oh. So, why didn't you call me at home later?
Patrick	Well, I forgot. Sorry.

> **Memo**
> Always look at the person you are speaking to. Don't look down at the page!

Exercise 3

Practice the conversation a few more times. Each time, use different excuses.

38

Look at page 42
Language fo

Listening task

Exercise 1 47

Listen to the conversation and circle Jonathan's excuses.

Exercise 2 47

Listen to the conversation once more and make a note of each of Jonathan's excuses.

Exercise 3 47

Listen to the conversation one more time. Check (✓) the excuse if Mrs. Fenway believes it or make an "✗" on the excuse if she does not believe it.

Speaking task one

You are a teacher. Student B is a student. Ask Student B questions. Write down Student B's excuses.

Example

Student A   Why didn't you finish the test yesterday?
Student B   I couldn't remember the answers.

Student B did not ...   **Student B's excuse:**

• finish the test yesterday.

• come to class on Monday.

• bring any books to class today.

• come to class on time.

• finish writing the book report.

• do the homework.

You are a teenager. Student B is your parent. Listen to each question and give Student B an excuse. (Use "I couldn't ..." or "I had to ..." with the cues below.)

• find the vacuum cleaner.
• study for an English test.
• pick up the garbage can. It was too heavy!
• find the dog food.
• (Make up your own excuse.)
• (Make up your own excuse.)

Do this exercise with everyone.

You did not do any of the six things below. Write down a reason for each thing you did not do. Then walk around the classroom and ask for and give reasons for each one. Write down the name of one person who has a *similar* reason next to each one.

You did not ...	Your reason:	Name:
• go bowling Friday night.		
• go swimming on Saturday.		
• go to the big party Saturday night.		
• play ball Sunday morning.		
• go shopping on Sunday.		
• go to a movie Sunday night.		

Speaking task two
Do this exercise in a group of three or more students.

Exercise 1

Student A
Write "Y" for "yes" next to any eight pictures and write "N" for "no" next to the other eight pictures.

Students B and C
Write the numbers of all the pictures (1–16) in random order on your chart below.

1

16

2

15

3

14

4

13

5

12

6   7  8   9   10   11

Exercise 2

Students B and C
Take turns asking Student A about the activities in your chart. Circle (O) numbers whenever Student A answers "yes" and cross off (✗) numbers whenever Student A answers "no."

Student A
Answer questions "yes" or "no" as marked above ("Y" or "N") and *give a reason* when you answer "no."

Continue until all the numbers are marked. Each time you get four "Os" or four "✗s" in a line, shout "Bingo!" The student with the most "bingos" wins!

Example

| **Student B** | Did you go to school last Friday? | **Student C** | Did you fix your bicycle yesterday? |
| **Student A** | Yes, I did. | **Student A** | No, I didn't. I couldn't find the tools. |

Homework

None of the people below (1–6) went to Mike's birthday party. Look at their thoughts and write each person's reason. (Make up a reason for Jason.)

Example

(Christine) I had to go to a wedding.

Christine

> **Memo**
> Write the reasons on a separate sheet of paper.

1 Ann

2 William

3 Chris

4 Ellen

5 Olivia

6 Jason

Homework review   Do this exercise with everyone.

Walk around and talk to your classmates. Take turns asking and answering why each person did not go to the party. For numbers 1–5, find someone who wrote the *same* reason that you wrote and write that person's name next to your sentence. For number 6, find someone who wrote a *similar* reason.

> **Memo**
> • Do this exercise in the next lesson if you have time.
> • If you cannot find anyone, write "no one."

Example

Student A   Why didn't Christine go to Mike's party?
Student B   She had to go to a wedding.

Language focus

Did you	fix the car?	→	I'm sorry.	I couldn't find the keys.
Why didn't you	clean the garage?		Sorry, but	I had to do a lot of homework.
				I didn't have time.
				I forgot.

42

8 COULDN'T AGREE MORE

Giving opinions

Warm-up exercises

Exercise 1

Write the man's reply and the woman's reply.

I think the city is great.

Exercise 2 48

Listen to the following conversation. Then practice it with *two* other students.

Tim	I don't think surprise quizzes are fair.
Eri	Right, I agree with you, Tim.
Jay	Actually, I think they're OK. In fact, I enjoy them!
Tim	In my opinion, all tests are useless.
Eri	I think so, too.
Jay	I don't think so. We study for tests, so we learn more.

> **Memo**
>
> Always look at the person you are speaking to. Don't look down at the page!

Exercise 3

Practice the conversation a few more times in groups of three. Each time, change roles and try to give the opinions, agree and disagree in different ways.

Look at page 48
Language focus

43

Listening task

 Exercise 1 49

Each picture shows an opinion. Listen to the conversation and write a number next to each picture to show the order that the opinions are given (1–3).

 Exercise 2 49

Listen to the conversation again and for each picture, circle (O) the name of the person who gives the opinion.

 Exercise 3 49

Listen again and check (✓) the names of the people who agree or disagree with each opinion.

Whose opinion?	Rob	John	Emma	Megan
Who agrees?				
Who disagrees?				

Whose opinion?	Rob	John	Emma	Megan
Who agrees?				
Who disagrees?				

Whose opinion?	Rob	John	Emma	Megan
Who agrees?				
Who disagrees?				

Speaking task one

Exercise 1 Do this exercise alone.

Match each opinion on page 45 with a reason to agree below.

The air is dirty and there's too much noise.

You can buy things anytime, anywhere.

Animals shouldn't be kept in cages.

It has a bad effect on young people.

They are bad for the country's health.

It's wrong to ignore them.

There's nothing to do and there's no privacy.

It would help to improve international relations.

The government should provide free education for everyone.

It helps you to see your own country and culture more clearly.

Exercise 2 Do this exercise alone.

Match each opinion on page 45 with a reason to disagree below.

It's so difficult. I think learning *one* is enough.

There's so much to do—such as going to plays and the opera, and visiting museums and art galleries.

You can learn just as much traveling around your *own* country.

It's too easy to spend more than you have.

They only put on what people want to watch.

It gives parents and students more choice.

Helping them find jobs and their own places to live is more important.

They are not *all* terrible. Some serve good food.

The animals are usually treated very well.

People are friendly and there's less crime.

Exercise 3 Do this exercise in a group of three students.

Student A
Tell each opinion (page 45) to your partners. Then listen as Student B agrees and Student C disagrees, and make sure their reasons are correct.

Student B
(Look only at this page.)
Listen to Student A's opinions. Agree with each one and give a reason from Exercise 1.

Student C
(Look only at this page.)
Listen to Student A's opinions. Disagree with each one and give a reason from Exercise 2.

Example

Student A   I think zoos are cruel places.
Student B   That's true. I believe that animals shouldn't be kept in cages.
Student C   Actually, I think the animals are usually treated very well.

Memo
- In Exercise 3, give opinions, agree and disagree in different ways.
- Change roles and do Exercise 3 again.

Speaking task two   Do this exercise in a group of three students.

Decide who is Student A, B and C. Write each topic in your list at the top of a box below (1–5). Make up a topic for box 6. Then take turns interviewing each other about the topics. Make notes of your partners' answers in each box.

Student A
Interview Student B and Student C about these topics:

1   watching sports on TV
2   foreign movies
3   loud parties
4   traveling by bus
5   learning to speak English
6   (Make up a topic.)

Student B
Interview Student A and Student C about these topics:

1   TV game shows
2   the Internet
3   surprise parties
4   traveling by train
5   doing English homework
6   (Make up a topic.)

Student C
Interview Student A and Student B about these topics:

1   TV talk shows
2   video games
3   karaoke parties
4   traveling by plane
5   this group work exercise
6   (Make up a topic.)

Example	
Student A	Keiko, what do you think about watching sports on TV?
Student B	I think it's a waste of time.
Student A	Do you agree, Juan?
Student C	No, I think it's a great way to relax.

Memo

- Students who are answering questions should close the book.

- Don't just say you like or dislike something. Give an opinion and your reasons for it.

1

2

3

4

5

6

Homework

For each opinion below, write a reply. Agree and give a reason or disagree and give a reason.

Memo

Write the replies on a separate sheet of paper.

Example

I agree. We have too many things to do at home.

1

I don't think teachers should give a lot of homework.

2

I think all airplanes should have a smoking section.

3

In my opinion, people should not ride bicycles in the park.

4

I don't think people should bring baby strollers into the subway.

5

I think that beaches should not allow people to play music.

6

I believe that taxis should pick up people with pets.

Homework review   Do this exercise with everyone.

Walk around and talk to your classmates. Take turns giving opinions and replying. For each opinion, find someone who wrote a reply *similar* to yours and write that person's name next to your sentence.

Memo

- Do this exercise in the next lesson if you have time.
- If you cannot find anyone, write "no one."

Example

Student A	I don't think teachers should give a lot of homework.
Student B	I agree. We have too many things to do at home.

Language focus

I think (that) I believe (that) In my opinion,	smoking should not be allowed in public places.

I don't think (that) smoking should be allowed in public places.

Agree	Disagree	
I think so, too. That's true. I agree with you.	I don't think so. That's true, but … I disagree.	Smokers have rights, too.
I don't think so either.	I don't agree with you.	

9 BIGGER AND BETTER
Comparing things

Warm-up exercises

Exercise 1

Write the man's reply.

My dog is cuter than your dog.

Exercise 2 50

Listen to the following conversation. Then practice it with a partner.

> **Memo**
> Always look at the person you are speaking to. Don't look down at the page!

Kevin	Which do you like more, motorcycles or cars?
Amy	Well, a motorcycle is more dangerous than a car.
Kevin	True, but a car isn't as enjoyable as a motorcycle.
Amy	Maybe, but is a motorcycle as comfortable as a car?
Kevin	No, it's not. But it's cheaper and easier to park.
Amy	Yeah, but a car is better in bad weather.

Exercise 3

Practice the conversation a few more times. Each time, talk about two different vehicles.

sports car

pick-up truck

SUV

limousine

Look at page 54

Language focus

Listening task

Exercise 1   51–55

Listen to the conversations (1–5) and check (✓)
the correct picture—left or right—for each one.

1

2

3

4

5

Exercise 2 51–55

Listen again and below the pictures make a note of the comparisons made in each conversation, as well as
any other keywords.

Exercise 3   51–55

Complete each of the following sentences with a comparison. Then listen
to the conversations again to check your answers.

> **M e m o**
>
> In Exercise 3 you can use your
> own words in the comparisons.

1 The white ones are

2 The red one is

3 The one on the right is

4 The five-island cruise is

5 The woman thinks hers is

Speaking task one   Do these exercises with a partner.

Exercise 1

With your partner, look at the vocabulary box and decide which words can describe each item at the top of pages 51 and 52. Then add as many words as you can to the list that could also describe each item.

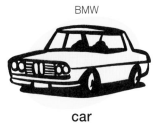
BMW

car

movie

restaurant

Exercise 2

Student A
Choose one of the groups on page 51 or 52, but do not tell Student B which one. Then answer Student B's questions in full sentences about comparisons of the items in your group with the items at the top.

Student B
Find out which group of pictures Student A has chosen by asking yes/no questions, comparing the items in the groups with the ones at the top (on pages 51 and 52).

> **Memo**
> Change roles and do Exercise 2 several times.

Group A

Group B

Group C

Group D

Vocabulary

• big	• comfortable	• exciting	• loud	• old	• roomy	• small
• busy	• crowded	• expensive	• modern	• popular	• scary	• soft
• cheap	• economical	• fast	• nice	• romantic	• slow	

office chair

chair

violin

instrument

ranch-style house

house

Example

| **Student B** | Is your car as expensive as a BMW? | **Student B** | Is your movie more romantic than *Star Wars*? |
| **Student A** | No, it's cheaper than a BMW. | **Student A** | Yes, it's more romantic. |

Memo

All questions should begin:

"Is your car/movie/ restaurant/chair/ instrument/house ... ?"

Group E

Group F

Group G

Group H

Speaking task two

Do Exercise 1 alone and Exercise 2 with everyone.

Exercise 1

Look at the differences between the two pictures. Choose six differences and write a comparison for each on the lines below.

Example

The yard was dirtier ten years ago.

> **Memo**
> Use "ten years ago" or "today" in your comparisons.

Granny Andrew Sarah Jack Martha

Ten years ago

Exercise 2

Walk around the class and exchange comparisons. For each one of your comparisons, find someone who made a *similar* comparison (about the same idea) and write his or her name next to your sentence.

Example

Student A	The yard was dirtier ten years ago.
Student B	Right, the yard's cleaner today.

> **Memo**
> In a large class find a *different* student for each comparison.

Today

Comparison:	Name:

Homework

Write three opinion questions and three factual questions, comparing two things in each question. See the box below for ideas for things to compare or use your own ideas.

IDEAS FOR COMPARISONS

- animals
- cities
- countries
- famous people
- food
- languages
- mountains
- music
- oceans
- rivers
- sports
- TV programs

Example

Opinion questions
- Which do you think is more interesting, rock music or jazz?
- Do you think soccer is more exciting than baseball?

Factual questions
- Is the Amazon River longer than the Mississippi River?
- Which is larger, Australia or the United States?

Homework review Do this exercise with everyone.

Walk around and talk to your classmates. Take turns asking and answering the questions.

- For each of your *opinion* questions, find someone who *agrees with you* and write that person's name next to your question.
- For each of your *factual* questions, find someone who *can answer it correctly* and write that person's name next to your question.

Language focus

The Volkswagen	is smaller than / is more economical than / isn't as comfortable as	the Cadillac.	
Is the Volkswagen	easier to park than / more popular than / as roomy as	the Cadillac?	Yes, it is. / I'm not sure. / No, it isn't.
Which is	faster, / more expensive,	the Volkswagen or the Cadillac?	The Cadillac (is).

54

Review exercises
Do these exercises with a partner.

Exercise 1

The teacher will give you one of the pictures (1–4) below. Each picture has the first line of a dialogue. Write two or more additional lines of dialogue for the picture.

1

Man Do you mind if I call the electrician?

2

Mother Is your new roommate better than your old one?

3

Old man I think all cell phones should be banned!

4

Woman Why didn't you bring the long rope?

Exercise 2

Say your lines to the class (with your partner). Do *not* say the first line of the dialogue above. The class will guess your picture.

Listening task

Exercise 1 56–60

Listen to the conversations (1–5) with your *book closed*. Then open your book and write the number of each conversation next to the correct picture.

Memo
- You can take notes as you listen.
- There is no conversation for one picture.

Exercise 2 56–60

Listen again and write the *keywords* next to each picture.

Memo

Keywords are important words that tell you which picture to choose.

Student B, turn to page 96

Speaking task one
Do Exercise 1 alone and Exercise 2 with a partner.

Exercise 1

Write a *comparison* for each picture (1–4).

1  ....

2  ....

3  ....

4  ....

Write a *request for permission* for each picture (5–8).

5  ....

6  ....

7  ....

8  ....

Exercise 2

Take turns with Student B guessing what each other wrote for each picture in Exercise 1. (Student B's pictures from Exercise 1 are below.)

The first one to guess all eight correctly wins!

> **Memo**
> - Each student can make only one guess per turn.
> - The wording does not have to be exactly the same.

Example

Student A	Did you write "A plane is faster than a bus"?	Student B	Did you write "Do you mind if I turn off the air conditioner"?
Student B	No, I didn't.	Student A	Yes, I did.

Comparisons

1   **2**  **3**   **4**

Requests for permission

5   **6**   **7**   **8**

Exercise 3   Do this exercise alone.

Fill in each blank (1–5) with a subject and then write your opinion about each subject.

1   Music: _____ (Fill in a type of music, a group or a song.)
subject

Opinion: ....

....

....

....

name / agree

name / disagree

2   Food: _____ (Fill in a type of food or a food item.)
subject

Opinion: ....

....

....

....

name / agree

name / disagree

3   Fashion: _____ (Fill in a fashion style or a clothing item.)
subject

Opinion: ....

....

....

....

name / agree

name / disagree

4   Movie or TV show: _____ (Fill in a title or a name.)
subject

Opinion: ....

....

....

....

name / agree

name / disagree

5   Transportation: _____ (Fill in a type of transportation.)
subject

Opinion: ....

....

....

....

name / agree

name / disagree

Exercise 4   Do this exercise with everyone.

Walk around the classroom and exchange opinions about the subjects you wrote about in Exercise 3.

- For each of your opinions, find one classmate who agrees and one who disagrees. Write each name.
- Listen to your classmates' opinions. Agree or disagree, and give a reason.

Speaking task two
Do this exercise in a group of three or more students.

The first student must choose a picture and say *why* he or she did not do it. The next student must repeat the sentence and then choose a different picture and make one more sentence. Each student must repeat *every* previous sentence and make one more sentence.

Continue around the circle and use as many pictures as possible, repeating *all* the sentence (with names) for about fifteen minutes (until your teacher says "stop").

The group of students that uses the most pictures, and correctly repeats the most sentences, wins!

Example

 James   I didn't exercise because I got up late.

    Yuko   James didn't exercise because he got up late. I didn't do laundry because I had to study.

    Kristin   James didn't exercise because he got up late. Yuko didn't do laundry because she had to study. I didn't call because I forgot.

    James   I didn't exercise because I got up late. Yuko didn't do laundry because she had to study. Kristin didn't call because she forgot. I didn't get a haircut because …

(continue)

Language game   Play this game with two to four "players" and one "caller."

Take turns choosing two numbers (1–24) from the grid below. Each number is a question or an answer. The caller will read each sentence that you choose.

Choose one number, listen to the caller read the sentence and then choose another number. Try to match a question with the answer. Do not write any notes. Just listen!

Continue until all the questions and answers have been matched. The player with the most matches wins!

> **Memo**
> • Cross off (✗) all matched numbers and circle *your* matches.
> • Look at this page only!
> • The teacher may let you write notes on the numbers.

Example

Player A	Number 4.		**Player B**	Number 23.
Caller	"Not at all, go ahead."		**Caller**	"Mind if I turn off the TV?"
Player A	Number 11.		**Player B**	Number 4.
Caller	"I wasn't invited!" They don't match!		**Caller**	"Not at all, go ahead." They match!

11 IF I WERE YOU
Giving advice and making suggestions

Warm-up exercises

Look at page 66

Exercise 1

Write the woman's reply.

Exercise 2 61

Listen to the following conversation. Then practice it with a partner.

> **Memo**
>
> Always look at the person you are speaking to. Don't look down at the page!

Rick	What's the matter, Greg?
Greg	I want to go fishing with friends on Sunday, but I have to work.
Rick	Why don't you tell your boss you have an upset stomach?
Greg	No, I couldn't do that.
Rick	Then you should just tell him you made plans.
Greg	Right, maybe I will.

Exercise 3

Practice the conversation a few more times. Each time, talk about a different plan and make a different suggestion.

Listening task

 Exercise 1 62

Listen to the conversation and circle the suggestions.

Exercise 2 62

Listen to the conversation again. Next to each of the suggestions, write a "✓" if Elizabeth accepts the idea, a "?" if she *may* accept the idea or an "✗" if she rejects the idea.

Speaking task one

Exercise 1

Student B has a problem.

- Listen to Student B and ask, "What's wrong?" or "What's the matter?"
- Then listen to Student B's problems and give Student B advice.

Choose advice to give Student B from the pictures below.

Example	
Student B	Oh, no!
Student A	What's the matter?
Student B	I lost my ATM card!
Student A	You'd better call the bank.

Exercise 2

You have a problem.

- Begin by saying something like "Oh, no!" or "Ohhh … !"
  Then tell Student B your problems (1–7).
- Write down Student B's advice next to each problem.

Example			
Student A	Ohhh … !	**Student A**	I left my camera on the train!
Student B	What's wrong?	**Student B**	Why don't you go to the "Lost and Found"?

1 You left your camera on the train.

2 You only slept two hours last night.

3 You lost your passport.

4 You have a cold and a sore throat.

5 You locked your keys in your car.

6 You have a toothache.

7 _____
   (Make up a problem.)

11

Exercise 3 Do this exercise with a partner.

Student A

First, tell Student B the name of a place that you know well. Then give Student B advice about where to stay, what to see, how to get around, etc., in that place.

Student B

Student A will tell you the name of a place that he or she knows well.

- Tell Student A that you are going to go to this place on vacation.
- Ask for Student A's advice about a good place to stay, places to go sightseeing, etc., and take notes about the place.

Memo

Change roles as Student A and Student B, and do the exercise again.

Example

| Student A | I grew up in Singapore. |
| Student B | Oh, really? I'm going there on vacation next summer! Listen, could you tell me … |

THINGS TO ASK ABOUT

- a good place to stay
- places to go sightseeing
- how to get around
- good places to eat
- things to do
- things to buy

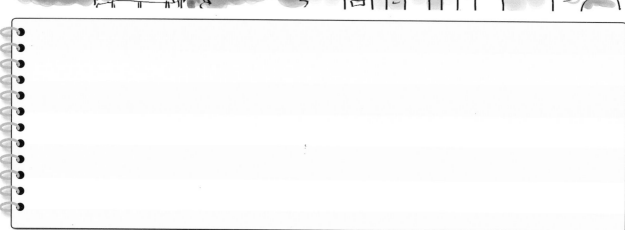

Speaking task two   Do Exercise 1 alone and Exercise 2 with everyone.

Exercise 1

Read what each person says and write down advice for that person below each picture.

Exercise 2

Walk around the classroom and talk to your classmates about each problem and your advice for each one. Next to each problem, write the name of any classmate with advice *similar* to yours.

Example

Student A	John bought a used car last week, and now it won't start.
Student B	He ought to take it to a repair shop.
Student A	If I were him, I'd …

> **Memo**
> - Keep changing partners.
> - Talk in pairs or small groups.

Sharon

....

....

....

Pete

....

....

....

Martin

....

....

....

John

....

....

....

Angela

....

....

....

Homework

Look at each couple's thoughts and write a suggestion for each dialogue. (Use "We should … ," "We ought to …" or "Why don't we … ?" for the suggestions.)

Memo

Write the suggestions on a separate sheet of paper.

1	**Husband**	It's our first wedding anniversary next month, honey! What shall we do to celebrate?
	Wife	[Makes a suggestion.]
	Husband	Well, it'll be expensive, but OK! Let's go!

2	**Wife**	Next week's our fifth anniversary. What do you want to do?
	Husband	[Makes a suggestion.]
	Wife	Sure, that sounds nice. Just the two of us.

3	**Wife**	It's our tenth anniversary this Friday. Do you want to do anything?
	Husband	[Makes a suggestion.]
	Wife	Yeah, OK. We haven't been out in a while.

4	**Wife**	Today's our twentieth anniversary … John? John!
	Husband	[Makes a suggestion.]
	Wife	OK. Is there anything good on?

Homework review Do this exercise with everyone.

Walk around and talk to your classmates. Read through the dialogues. For each dialogue, find someone who wrote a suggestion *similar* to yours and write that person's name next to your suggestion.

Memo

• Do this exercise in the next lesson if you have time.

• If you cannot find anyone, write "no one."

Language focus

| What's | wrong? | | I have a toothache. |
| | the matter? | | I lost my credit card. |

You should				I'm going to.
You ought to	go to the dentist.		Yes,	that's a good idea.
You'd better	call the credit card company.		Yeah,	I think I will.
Why don't you			Right,	maybe I will.
If I were you, I'd				I guess I should.

12 HAVE YOU EVER ... ?

Talking about experiences

Warm-up exercises

Write the woman's question.

  63

Listen to the following conversation. Then practice it with a partner.

> **Memo**
>
> Always look at the person you are
> speaking to. Don't look down at the page!

Katie	Have you ever been bungee jumping?
Hiro	No, I haven't. Have you?
Katie	Yeah, I went with my boyfriend last year.
Hiro	Where did you do it?
Katie	In Canada. Have you ever been there?
Hiro	Yes, I went to Quebec five years ago, on vacation.

Practice the conversation a few more times. Each time, ask about a different activity and make up the answers.

Look at page 72

Language focus

67

12

Listening task

Exercise 1 ⊙ 64 Do Exercise 1 alone.

Look at the pictures and then listen to the conversation with your book closed.
Then open your book and number the pictures in the correct order (1–6).

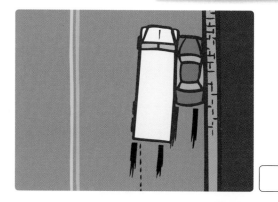

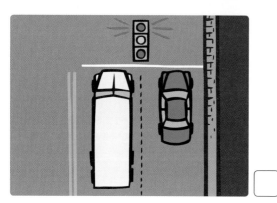

Exercise 2 ⊙ 64 Do Exercise 2 alone.

Listen again and write the *keywords* next to each picture.

Exercise 3 ⊙ 64 Do Exercise 3 with a partner.

Listen one more time and then take turns retelling the story with a partner (one as the storyteller and one as the listener).

Student B, turn to pages 99–100

Speaking task one

Exercise 1

Take turns with Student B asking and answering questions about the people on pages 69 and 70. (Look at the *Experiences* box on page 70 for help.)

- If you have a blank, ask Student B about the experience and write notes in the blank. First, ask a yes/no question. If the answer is "yes," ask the *Wh-* question.
- Answer Student B's questions with the information below the picture.

> **Memo**
> - At first answer only with "yes" or "no."
> - Have fun and *make up* answers about your own experiences for box number 4.

Example

Student A	Has Nicole ever been on a boat?
Student B	Yes, she has.
Student A	Who did she go with?
Student B	She went with her family.

| Student B | Has she ever met a famous person? |
| Student A | No, she hasn't. |

1

2

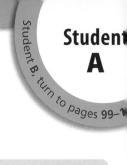

Exercise 2

Check your answers with your partner. Take turns and make full sentences for the experiences you have asked about.

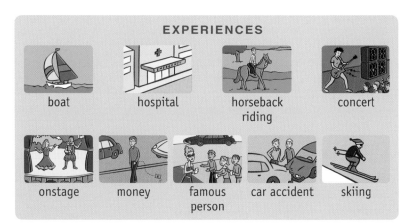

EXPERIENCES

boat   hospital   horseback riding   concert

onstage   money   famous person   car accident   skiing

Example

Student A Nicole's been on a boat. She went with her family.

Student B Nicole's never met a famous person.

3

Rob and Sophia

Why? — yes (their friend)
Who? — no

How much?
How? — yes (Tom Cruise)
Where?

yes (was in "Macbeth")

4

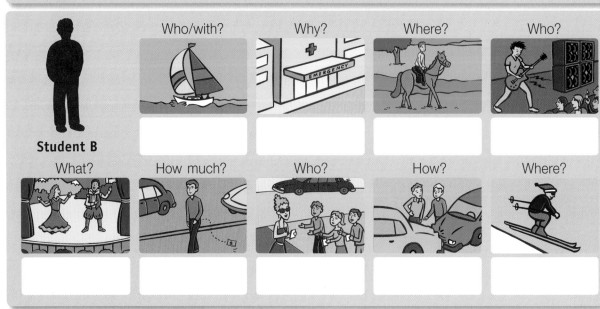

Student B

Who/with? Why? Where? Who?

What? How much? Who? How? Where?

Speaking task two
Do Exercise 1 alone and Exercise 2 with everyone.

Exercise 1

Choose three of the topics below and make up a "Have you ever … ?" question for each one. Write a topic and a specific question on each notepad on the right.

Example

Topic: a movie
Question: Have you ever seen "The Matrix"?

TOPICS

- a movie
- a strange experience
- music
- a job
- finding something
- losing something
- foreign travel
- (your own topic)

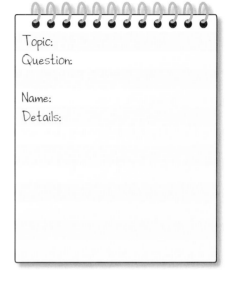

Topic:
Question:

Name:
Details:

Topic:
Question:

Name:
Details:

Exercise 2

Ask around the class and, for each question, find someone who answers "yes" and write down his or her name. Then ask a few more questions about the experience and write down the details (*when*, *where*, *why*, etc.).

Memo

- Talk to three different people.
- Take turns asking and answering questions.

Topic:
Question:

Name:
Details:

Exercise 3   (Optional)

The teacher may call on you to tell the class about one of the experiences you have asked about. Look at your notes on the details of the experience and tell the class the story.

Homework

Write a "Have you ever ... ?" question for each of the six pictures.

Example

Have you ever won a contest?

1

2

3

4

5

6

Homework review Do this exercise with everyone.

Walk around and talk to your classmates. Take turns asking and answering each other's questions. For each one find someone who answers "yes" and ask a few *Wh-* questions for more information. Write that person's name with a note about the information next to your question.

Language focus

Have you ever	gone surfing? ridden a camel? been to Hawaii?	→	Yes, I have. No, I haven't.

When		go?	→	I went last summer.
Where	did you	ride one?	→	I rode one in Egypt.
Who		go with?	→	I went with my friends.

13 HOW ABOUT DINNER?

Inviting

Warm-up exercises

Exercise 1

Write the woman's answer.

How about going for a ride in my airplane?

Exercise 2 🔊 65

Listen to the following conversation. Then practice it with a partner.

Memo

Always look at the person you are speaking to. Don't look down at the page!

Lena	Hi, Jade. Listen, would you like to see a movie tonight?
Jade	I'm sorry, but I have to babysit.
Lena	Oh. Then how about tomorrow night?
Jade	Yeah, that sounds great. Let's go tomorrow!
Lena	Great! Let's meet at the bus stop after school.
Jade	Sure, OK.

Exercise 3

Practice the conversation a few more times. Each time, use a different invitation and refuse for a different reason.

Look at page 77
Language focus

Listening task

Exercise 1 66

Listen to the conversation and circle all the things that
Zachary invites Mia to do.

Exercise 2 66

Listen again and make an "✗" on the invitations that Mia
refuses and check (✓) the one that she accepts.

Exercise 3 66

Listen once more and draw a square around *each reason* that Mia gives Zachary when she refuses and
match the reason with the invitation.

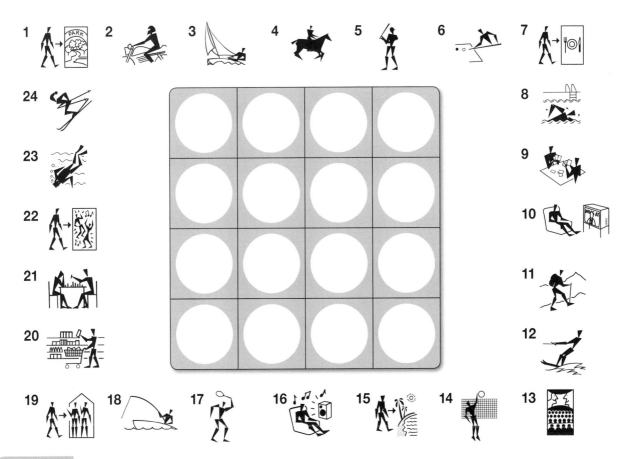

Speaking task one Do Exercise 1 alone and Exercise 2 with a partner.

Exercise 1

Write the numbers of any sixteen of the activities (1–24) in random order on your chart below. Then write "A" for "accept" next to any twelve pictures and write "R" for "refuse" next to the other twelve pictures.

Memo
Do not show your page to your partner.

Exercise 2

Take turns inviting each other to do the sixteen activities on your charts.

- Invite your partner and circle (O) any activity on your chart that your partner accepts and cross off (✗) any activity on your chart that your partner refuses.
- Accept or refuse each invitation (as marked "A" or "R" above) and *give a reason* when you refuse.

Continue until all your chart numbers are marked. Each time you get four "Os" or four "✗s" in a line, shout "Bingo!" The student with the most "bingos" wins!

Memo
Only circle (O) or cross off (✗) numbers on your chart when you *invite*, not when you answer.

Example

| Student A | Would you like to go to the park on Friday? | Student B | How about playing tennis on Sunday? |
| Student B | Sure, I'd love to. | Student A | I'm sorry, but I have to work on Sunday. |

Speaking task two
Do Exercise 1 alone and Exercise 2 with everyone.

Exercise 1

Fill in any five mornings, five afternoons and five evenings on the schedule below with different activities—things that you have to do or dates that you have. (Choose from the activities on the right or make up your own.)

	Monday	Tuesday	Wednesday	Thursday	Friday	Saturday	Sunday
Morning							
Afternoon							
Evening							

Exercise 2

Walk around the classroom and make dates with four different people:

- one person in the morning
- one person in the afternoon
- one person in the evening
- one person at any time

You can only make a date for a time you are free. For each date that you make (or accept), write on your schedule:

- who you will meet
- the activity (Choose from below or make up your own.)

Example

Student A	Would you like to go to a movie Friday night?
Student B	I'm sorry, but I have to work.
Student A	Then how about Saturday night?
Student B	Sure, that sounds great.

⑬

Homework

Write the lines of the dialogue *in order*, and begin each line with "Charlie" or "Diane." (Charlie's lines are in blue boxes.) Line numbers 3, 8 and 11 have been marked.

Memo

Write the dialogue on a separate sheet of paper.

Good. How about seeing *The Final Battle*?

Oh, then how about Saturday night?

Well, listen, Charlie, would you like to go to a movie Sunday night?

Hello?

A concert? Oh, then maybe another time …

3   I'd love to, but I have to work in the afternoon.

8   That's a great idea.

Hi, Diane, it's Charlie. How about going to a movie on Saturday afternoon?

I'm sorry, but Saturday night I'm going to a concert with Sue.

Sure, six o'clock is fine.

That sounds great. Where shall we meet?

11   How about meeting at the mall around six o'clock?

Homework review   Do this exercise with a partner.

Practice the dialogue with a partner and make sure all your lines are in the correct order.

Memo

- Do this exercise in the next lesson if you have time.
- Always look at your partner when you are speaking.

Language focus

Would you like to	go to a movie tonight?
How about Do you feel like	going to the beach tomorrow?

Accept	Refuse	
I'd love to. That sounds great. That's a great idea.	I'd love to, but That sounds great, but I'm sorry, but	I have to study for a test.

77

14 IT'S GONNA RAIN
Making predictions

Warm-up exercises

Exercise 1

Write the prediction of the second fortune-teller.

You're going to meet a woman with blonde hair …

Exercise 2 67

Listen to the following conversation. Then practice it with *two* other students.

Ron	I'm sure Argentina will win.
Dan	Yeah, they're definitely going to win!
Emily	I don't know. Maybe they'll win.
[*later*]	
Ron	Argentina is definitely going to lose.
Dan	Yeah, they're going to lose.
Emily	I'm not sure. They might lose.

> **Memo**
>
> Always look at the person you are speaking to. Don't look down at the page!

Exercise 3

Practice the conversation a few more times in groups of three. Each time, make different predictions about the game.

Look at page 82 Language fo…

Listening task

Exercise 1 68

Listen to the conversation and circle any picture that represents a prediction that you hear.

Exercise 2 68

Listen to the conversation again. Next to each of the predictions, write a "✓" if the person is certain and a "?" if the person is not sure.

Exercise 3 68

Listen once more and make a note of each prediction.

Speaking task one Do this exercise with a partner.

Student A
For each question below make a prediction about Student B's future. Check (✓) if Student B agrees or disagrees with you.

Student B
Listen to Student A's predictions and tell Student A if you agree or disagree.

Memo
- Student B: Close your book. Answer truthfully.
- Change roles as Student A and Student B, and do the exercise again.

Example		Agrees	Disagrees
Student A	I think you'll definitely be a student at this school next year.	✓	☐
Student B	You're right, I will.		
Student A	I think you might be a student at this school next year.	☐	✓
Student B	No, I don't think so.		
Student A	I don't think you'll be a student at this school next year.	✓	☐
Student B	I don't think so either.		

Do you think your partner will ...

	Agrees	Disagrees
... be a student at this school next year?	☐	☐
... study a foreign language besides English someday?	☐	☐
... go overseas to study someday?	☐	☐
... get a new job within five years?	☐	☐
... move to a new home within five years?	☐	☐
... buy a motorcycle someday?	☐	☐
... get married within ten years?	☐	☐
... have grandchildren someday?	☐	☐
... go overseas on vacation in the near future?	☐	☐
... live in another country some time in the future?	☐	☐
... be famous someday?	☐	☐
... _____ (Make your own prediction.)	☐	☐
Total:	☐	☐

Speaking task two

Do Exercise 1 in a group of three or four students, and Exercise 2 with everyone.

Memo

Make predictions in different ways, using "going to," "will," "maybe," "might," etc.

Exercise 1

Talk about life in the future with your group and make some predictions. (See the *Topics* box for ideas or use your own ideas.) Each member of your group must choose a different prediction to write down. Write your prediction in the box below.

Example

We'll probably fly everywhere in 100 years.

Prediction

TOPICS

- the environment
- space travel
- transportation
- communication
- shopping
- computers
- language
- homes
- school
- work
- (your own idea)

Exercise 2

Memo

The teacher may ask you to present the results of your survey to the class.

Go around the classroom and tell your prediction to the other students and listen to their predictions. Agree or disagree with other students' predictions, and if you *disagree*, give your own opinion. Make a check (✓) in a box below when a classmate agrees or disagrees with your prediction.

Example

Student A	We'll probably fly everywhere in 100 years.	Student C	We'll carry computers with us everywhere.
Student B	I don't think so. I think we'll still use cars.	Student D	Yes, I think we will, too.

Agrees	Disagrees

Homework

Write four predictions for the coming days, months or year about current events in the news (See the *Topics* box below.).

Example

- It is going to rain tomorrow.
- I think Brazil will win the World Cup this year.

TOPICS

- the weather
- sports news
- a famous person in the news
- politics (elections or politicians)
- crime (criminal acts or court trials)
- international news stories

Homework review   Do this exercise with everyone.

Walk around and talk to your classmates. Take turns telling each other predictions.

- For each of your predictions, try to find someone who made a *similar* prediction and write that person's name next to your prediction.
- For each prediction you hear, say if you agree or disagree with the prediction.

Language focus

I'm sure they'll They're definitely going to	
They'll They're going to	win the game on Sunday. come tonight.
I think they'll They'll probably	call us later. be late tomorrow.
Maybe they'll They *could* They might	

15 SAY THAT AGAIN
Review and consolidation

Review exercises   Do these exercises with a partner.

Memo
- Write on a separate sheet of paper.
- If you finish early, write an answer for *another* picture.

Exercise 1

The teacher will give you one of the pictures (1–4) below. Each picture has the first line of a dialogue. Write two or more additional lines of dialogue for the picture.

1

Driver   Uh-oh. I think we ran out of gas.

2

Man   Hello, Lauren? Would you like to come over and see my new spider?

3

Passenger   Have you ever met a movie star?

4

Husband   Honey? Let's have lunch outside. I think it's going to be a beautiful afternoon!

Exercise 2

Say your lines to the class (with your partner). Do *not* say the first line of the dialogue above. The class will guess your picture.

Memo
Try to memorize your lines for Exercise 2.

Listening task

Exercise 1   69–73

Listen to the conversations (1–5) with your *book closed*. Then open your book and write the number of each conversation next to the correct picture.

Exercise 2 69–73

Listen again and write the *keywords* next to each picture.

Student B, turn to page 101

Speaking task one

Exercise 1

Give Student B clues for each answer in Crossword puzzle 1 until Student B guesses the answer. Use "blanks" in your clues. (You can give more than one clue for an answer.)

Memo

For help with clues, you can look at the unit shown for each word, but try to make up your own sentences.

Example

Student B	What's 1 down?
Student A	I "blank" with you. I think cats are smarter than dogs.
Student B	Disagree?
Student A	That's right!

Crossword puzzle 1

Unit 8: Giving opinions
Unit 3: Making requests
Unit 12: Talking about experiences
Unit 6: Asking for permission
Unit 8: Giving opinions
Unit 13: Inviting

Unit 9: Making comparisons

Unit 4: Giving instructions

Unit 7: Making excuses and giving reasons

Unit 13: Inviting

Crossword (across/down) answers:
1 DANGEROUS
5 TAKE
7 REMEMBER
9 LOVE
1 DISAGREE
2 EVER
3 OK
4 SURE
6 TRUE
8 MIND
7 REGRET

Exercise 2

Ask Student B for clues and fill in Crossword puzzle 2. In each clue, the "blank" in Student B's sentence is the answer.

Example

Student A	What's 1 down?
Student B	He's poor now, but I'm sure he'll be rich "blank."
Student A	Someday?
Student B	That's right!

Crossword puzzle 2

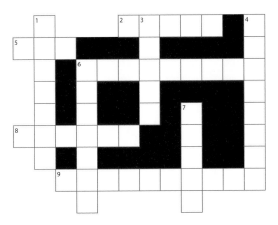

85

Speaking task two

Do this exercise in groups of three or four.

Student A

Tell the group a story about yourself. The story must be 100 percent true or 100 percent false. Do not tell the other students in your group if it is true or false. They will ask you questions about your story and then guess if it is true or false.

Students B, C and D

Listen to Student A's story and then ask questions about the story. Then tell Student A whether you think the story is true or false.

Memo

Each student take a turn as Student A and tell the group a story.

Language game

Play this game with two to four "players" and one "caller."

Take turns choosing two numbers (1–20) from the grid below. Each number is a question or an answer. The caller will read each sentence that you choose.

Choose one number, listen to the caller read the sentence and then choose another number. Try to match a question with the answer. Do not write any notes. Just listen!

Continue until all the questions and answers have been matched. The player with the most matches wins!

Memo

All students should do Exercise 1 on page 102 first.

Memo

- Cross off (✗) all matched numbers and circle *your* matches.
- Look at this page only!
- The teacher may let you write notes on the numbers.

Example			
Player A	Number 4.	**Player B**	Number 11.
Caller	"Sure, go ahead."	**Caller**	"Can I close the door?"
Player A	Number 20.	**Player B**	Number 4.
Caller	"Is it big?" They don't match!	**Caller**	"Sure, go ahead." They match!

APPENDIX

STUDENT B PAGES

Getting Started	She lives in Yokohama.	90
Unit 1	It leaves at ten o'clock.	91
	Could you tell me the best time of the year to visit Greece?	92
Unit 5	Put in the money and press this button.	93
Unit 6	I'm sorry, but I have to use it this weekend.	94
Unit 7	I couldn't find the vacuum cleaner.	95
Unit 10	Mind if I open the door?	96
	What do you think of life in New York?	97
Unit 11	What's wrong?	98
Unit 12	Has Nicole ever been on a boat?	99
Unit 15	What's 1 down?	101
	Can I close the door?	102

SELF-STUDY EXERCISES

Unit 1	Downloadable tracks 1–8	103
Unit 2	Downloadable tracks 9–14	104
Unit 3	Downloadable tracks 15 and 16	105
Unit 4	Downloadable tracks 17–22	106
Unit 6	Downloadable tracks 23–26	107
Unit 7	Downloadable track 27	108
Unit 8	Downloadable tracks 28 and 29	109
Unit 9	Downloadable tracks 30–39	110
Unit 11	Downloadable track 40	111
Unit 12	Downloadable tracks 41 and 42	112
Unit 13	Downloadable track 43	113
Unit 14	Downloadable tracks 44 and 45	114

SELF-STUDY EXERCISES ANSWER KEY | 115

AUDIO SCRIPT | 117

Speaking task one

Exercise 1

Look at the information and answer Student A's questions.

Student A, turn to page 4

Memo
- Answer in *full* sentences.
- Change roles as Student A and Student B, and do the exercises again.

Example

Student A	Where does Jenny live?	**Student A**	What does she do?
Student B	She lives in Yokohama.	**Student B**	She's a waitress.

1 Personal information: Jenny Chang

Lives in: Yokohama

Occupation: Waitress

Languages: Korean and Japanese

Hobbies: Yoga and gardening

2 Personal information: Carlos Lopez

Lives in: London

Occupation: Taxi driver

Languages: Spanish and English

Hobbies: Chess and soccer

3 Personal information: Ken and Pat Lee

Live in: Hong Kong

Occupations: Students

Languages: Chinese and English

Hobbies: Tennis and surfing

Exercise 2

Answer Student A's questions about your personal information. You can *make up* the information, if you like.

Student A, turn to page 7

Student B

Speaking task one

Exercise 1

You are a travel agent. Look at the information for flights and buses and answer Student A's questions. (Find out what time Student A would like to leave.)

Memo

Change roles as Student A and Student B, and do the exercises again.

Example

Student B	Can I help you?
Student A	Yes, I'd like to go to Chicago.
Student B	How would you like to travel?
Student A	I'm not sure. I'd like some information on the buses and flights.
Student B	OK, I can help you.
Student A	Great! Could you tell me … ?

Bus information: New York to Chicago				
Bus number	Departs	Arrives	Duration	Fare
3209	3:15 p.m.	11:00 a.m. next day	20 hrs. 45 mins.	$91
3211	4:40 p.m.	11:05 a.m. next day	19 hrs. 25 mins.	$91
3213	6:20 p.m.	1:40 p.m. next day	20 hrs. 20 mins.	$91
3217	8:50 p.m.	3:25 p.m. next day	19 hrs. 35 mins.	$91

Flight information: New York to Chicago				
Flight number	Departs	Arrives	Flight time	Fare
305	7:00 a.m.	8:32 a.m.	2 hrs. 32 mins.	$249
313	9:00 a.m.	10:36 a.m.	2 hrs. 36 mins.	$267
321	11:00 a.m.	12:24 p.m.	2 hrs. 24 mins.	$267
328	12:35 p.m.	2:00 p.m.	2 hrs. 25 mins.	$267
333	2:00 p.m.	3:27 p.m.	2 hrs. 27 mins.	$267
345	4:59 p.m.	6:31 p.m.	2 hrs. 32 mins.	$267
405	6:30 p.m.	8:00 p.m.	2 hrs. 30 mins.	$249
413	8:05 p.m.	9:37 p.m.	2 hrs. 32 mins.	$249

Exercise 2

You are the manager of a language school. Student A wants to take a language course. Answer Student A's questions. Make up the answers!

Example

Student A	Could you tell me if you have a Chinese language course?
Student B	Yes, we do.
Student A	OK, could you tell me … ?

Speaking task two Do this exercise with everyone.

The teacher will divide the class into two halves, Group A and Group B, and give each student in Group B some of the information boxes below. Answer Group A's questions, but answer *only* the questions that you have information to answer. For all other questions, answer, "I'm sorry, I don't know."

Example

Student A	Do you know how long it takes to go from England to France by ferry?
Student B	Yes, it takes one and a half hours.

Student A	Could you tell me the best month to travel through Australia?
Student B	I'm sorry, I don't know.

Memo
- Check (✓) the boxes the teacher gives you.
- Do not show your boxes to anyone!
- Group B students may stay in their seats.

1 A train ticket from Tokyo to Osaka costs about $225.

2 Two places to visit in San Francisco are the Golden Gate Bridge and Fisherman's Wharf.

3 It takes about 3½ hours to fly from Australia to New Zealand.

4 The best way to travel from Hong Kong to Macau is by hydrofoil, the fastest ferry.

5 Two places to visit in Athens are the Plaka and the Parthenon.

6 It's cold in Australia in July. (It's winter!)

7 Spring is the best time of year to visit Greece.

8 It costs about $11 to see a movie in London.

9 The cheapest way to travel from New York to California is by bus.

10 Spring is the best season to trek in the Himalayas.

11 Most of the subways in Tokyo stop running about one o'clock in the morning.

12 It costs about $60 to take a horse-and-buggy ride in Central Park in New York City.

13 The banks in Hong Kong open at nine o'clock in the morning.

14 A ferry ticket costs about $90 one way from England to France.

15 It costs about $450 round trip for a cheap flight from New York to London.

16 Most of the shops in Barcelona are closed for *siesta* from 1:30 to 3:30 in the afternoon.

17 It takes about 1½ hours to go from England to France by ferry.

18 It's very hot in Thailand in January.

19 A cup of coffee costs about $5.50 at a sidewalk café in Paris.

20 It takes about 7½ hours to fly from New York to London.

21 It takes about 2½ hours to go from Tokyo to Osaka by train.

22 It's hot and rainy in India in August.

23 January is the best month to travel through Australia.

24 Two places to visit in Beijing are the Great Wall and the Forbidden City.

Player, turn to page 31

Language game   Play this game with two to four "players" and one "caller."

Before you begin the game, number the questions and answers below from 1 to 24 in *random order* (all mixed up).

The players will take turns choosing two numbers. Listen for the first number and read the first sentence. Listen for the second number, read the second sentence and say if it matches the first sentence or not.* After that, the next player chooses.

Continue until all the questions and answers are matched. The player with the most matches wins!

*You can also ask the players if it is a match before you tell them.

> **Memo**
> - Read each sentence slowly, once or twice.
> - Read both of the sentences *before* you say, "They match!" or "They don't match!"

Example

Player A	Number 4.	**Player B**	Number 23.
Caller	"Could you lend me your pen?"	**Caller**	"Of course. Here you are."
Player A	Number 11.	**Player B**	Number 4.
Caller	"Is it big?" They don't match!	**Caller**	"Could you lend me your pen?" They match!

Question

- ( ) Could you lend me your pen?
- ( ) Could you tell me how long the trip is?
- ( ) What does your jacket look like?
- ( ) How do you use this ticket machine?
- ( ) Do you know what time it leaves?
- ( ) What's that made of?
- ( ) Does he know how to ski?
- ( ) Do you think you could give me a ride?
- ( ) Where can I cash traveler's checks?
- ( ) Do you know how to close this?
- ( ) Would you mind calling me back later?
- ( ) Is it big?

Answer

- ( ) Of course. Here you are.
- ( ) It takes about 48 hours.
- ( ) Well, it's plaid, and it has black buttons.
- ( ) Put in the money and press this button.
- ( ) Every hour on the hour.
- ( ) Mostly glass, but this part's plastic.
- ( ) Yes, he does. He goes skiing every winter.
- ( ) Sure, no problem. It's on my way home.
- ( ) There's a bank around the corner.
- ( ) Yeah, just turn it clockwise.
- ( ) Not at all. I'll call around five o'clock.
- ( ) No, it's small enough to fit in your pocket.

Student A, turn to page 34

Speaking task one

Exercise 1

You are a college student. Student A is your roommate. Look at the information below. Answer Student A's requests. (You can give *or* refuse permission.)

Student A is a great roommate. You usually say "yes" to Student A's requests, but remember these things:

- You are going to drive a friend to the airport on Friday night.
- You have to watch a documentary on TV tonight for History class.
- You are going to take pictures at a friend's wedding on Sunday.

Exercise 2

You are an office worker. Student A is your boss. Ask Student A for permission to:

	Check (✓): Permission	
	given	refused
take a thirty-minute break to go to the bank.	☐	☐
take this Friday off.	☐	☐
come to work an hour late on Monday.	☐	☐
take a two-hour lunch break tomorrow.	☐	☐
make a personal overseas phone call.	☐	☐
use the company car over the weekend.	☐	☐
get a new telephone.	☐	☐
take a four-week vacation this summer.	☐	☐

Example

Student B	Is it OK if I come to work an hour late on Monday?
Student A	I'm sorry, but …

Exercise 3

You are a teacher. Student A is your student. Look at the information below. Answer Student A's requests. (You can give *or* refuse permission.)

Student A is a good student. You usually say "yes" to Student A's requests, but remember these things:

- You do not like it when students come to class late.
- You do not let students leave early unless it is an emergency.
- You do not want Student A to miss any classes.

Exercise 4

You are a teenager. Student A is your parent. Ask Student A if you can:

	Check (✓): Permission	
	given	refused
invite a friend to dinner.	☐	☐
get a part-time job in the evening.	☐	☐
go on a camping trip with friends.	☐	☐
buy a small motorcycle.	☐	☐
sleep at a friend's house this weekend.	☐	☐
paint your bedroom black and white.	☐	☐
have a party next weekend.	☐	☐
go to France for the summer with friends.	☐	☐

Student A, turn to page 40

Speaking task one

Exercise 1

You are a student. Student A is your teacher. Listen to each question and give Student A an excuse. (Use "I couldn't …" or "I had to …" with the cues below.)

Example

Student A	Why didn't you finish the test yesterday?
Student B	I couldn't remember the answers.

* remember the answers.
* visit my aunt in the hospital.
* open my locker.
* go to the dentist this morning.
* (Make up your own excuse.)
* (Make up your own excuse.)

Exercise 2

You are Student A's parent. Student A is a teenager. Ask Student A questions. Write down Student A's excuses.

Student A did not …	Student A's excuse:
• clean the basement.	
• do the laundry.	
• take out the garbage.	
• feed the dog.	
• wash the dishes.	
• get a haircut.	

Exercise 3   Do this exercise with everyone.

You did not do any of the six things below. Write down a reason for each thing you did not do. Then walk around the classroom and ask for and give reasons for each one. Write down the name of one person who has a *similar* reason next to each one.

You did not …	Your reason:	Name:
• go bowling Friday night.		
• go swimming on Saturday.		
• go to the big party Saturday night.		
• play ball Sunday morning.		
• go shopping on Sunday.		
• go to a movie Sunday night.		

Speaking task one

Do Exercise 1 alone and Exercise 2 with a partner.

Exercise 1

Write a *comparison* for each picture (1–4).

1  ....

2  ....

3  ....

4  ....

Write a *request for permission* for each picture (5–8).

5  ....

6  ....

7  ....

8  ....

Exercise 2

Take turns with Student A guessing what each other wrote for each picture in Exercise 1. (Student A's pictures from Exercise 1 are below.)

The first one to guess all eight correctly wins!

Memo

- Each student can make only one guess per turn.
- The wording does not have to be exactly the same.

Example

| **Student A** | Did you write "A plane is faster than a bus"? | **Student B** | Did you write "Do you mind if I turn off the air conditioner"? |
| **Student B** | No, I didn't. | **Student A** | Yes, I did. |

Comparisons

1 **2** **3** **4**

Requests for permission

5 **6**  **7** **8**

Player, turn to page 60

Caller

Language game   Play this game with two to four "players" and one "caller."

Before you begin the game, number the questions and answers below from 1 to 24 in *random order* (all mixed up).

The players will take turns choosing two numbers. Listen for the first number and read the first sentence. Listen for the second number, read the second sentence and say if it matches the first sentence or not.* After that, the next player chooses.

Continue until all the questions and answers are matched. The player with the most matches wins!

*You can also ask the players if it is a match before you tell them.

> **Memo**
> - Read each sentence slowly, once or twice.
> - Read both of the sentences *before* you say, "They match!" or "They don't match!"

Example

Player A	Number 4.		**Player B**	Number 23.
Caller	"Not at all, go ahead."		**Caller**	"Mind if I turn off the TV?"
Player A	Number 11.		**Player B**	Number 4.
Caller	"I wasn't invited!" They don't match!		**Caller**	"Not at all, go ahead." They match!

Question	Answer
◯ Can I use your calculator for a minute?	◯ Of course, it's on the table over there.
◯ Why didn't you hand in the homework?	◯ I'm sorry, but my cat tore it up.
◯ What do you think of life in New York?	◯ It can be dangerous, but I love it!
◯ Is this house larger than yours?	◯ Actually, I think it's smaller.
◯ Mind if I turn off the TV?	◯ Not at all, go ahead.
◯ Why didn't you clean your room?	◯ Well, I couldn't find the vacuum cleaner.
◯ The new mayor's great, isn't he?	◯ Actually, I'm not sure about him.
◯ Is the Nile longer than the Mississippi?	◯ Sure, it's about 1,800 miles longer.
◯ Could I possibly use your car tonight?	◯ I'm sorry, but it has two flat tires.
◯ Why weren't you at my surprise party?	◯ I wasn't invited!
◯ I think TV's bad for children, don't you?	◯ Well, I think that too much can be harmful.
◯ Is your dog friendlier than your cat?	◯ Yeah, but my cat's smarter.

Student A, turn to page 63

Studen[t]
B

Speaking task one

Exercise 1

You have a problem.

Memo
- Make up one problem (number 7).
- The teacher may give you different expressions to begin your conversation.

- Begin by saying something like "Oh, no!" or "Ohhh … !" Then tell Student A your problems (1–7).
- Write down Student A's advice next to each problem.

Example

| Student B | Oh, no! | Student B | I lost my ATM card! |
| Student A | What's the matter? | Student A | You'd better call the bank. |

1   You lost your ATM card.
2   You have stomach pain and a fever.
3   You have a big test on Monday.
4   Someone stole your bicycle!
5   You have a headache.
6   You left your wallet at a restaurant.
7   _____
     (Make up a problem.)

Exercise 2

Student A has a problem.

Memo
- Give advice in different ways.
- Make up your own advice for the last problem.

- Listen to Student A and ask, "What's wrong?" or "What's the matter?"
- Then listen to Student A's problems and give Student A advice.

Choose advice to give Student A from the pictures below.

Example

Student A	Ohhh … !
Student B	What's wrong?
Student A	I left my camera on the train!
Student B	Why don't you go to the "Lost and Found"?

Student A, turn to pages 69–70

Speaking task one

Exercise 1

Take turns with Student A asking and answering questions about the people on pages 99 and 100. (Look at the *Experiences* box on page 100 for help.)

- If you have a blank, ask Student A about the experience and write notes in the blank. First, ask a yes/no question. If the answer is "yes," ask the *Wh-* question.
- Answer Student A's questions with the information below the picture.

Memo

- At first answer only with "yes" or "no."
- Have fun and *make up* answers about your own experiences for box number 4.

Example

Student A	Has Nicole ever been on a boat?	Student B	Has she ever met a famous person?
Student B	Yes, she has.	Student A	No, she hasn't.
Student A	Who did she go with?		
Student B	She went with her family.		

99

Exercise 2

Check your answers with your partner.
Take turns and make full sentences for
the experiences you have asked about.

Example	
Student A	Nicole's been on a boat. She went with her family.
Student B	Nicole's never met a famous person.

EXPERIENCES

boat   hospital   horseback riding   concert

onstage   money   famous person   car accident   skiing

3

Rob and Sophia

Who/with?   yes (car accident)   Where?   no

What?   no   Who?   yes (drove too fast)   yes (Switzerland)

4

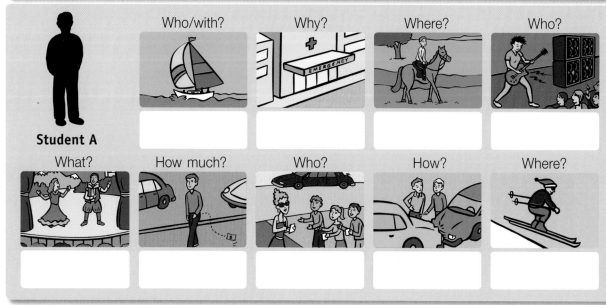

Student A

Who/with?   Why?   Where?   Who?

What?   How much?   Who?   How?   Where?

Speaking task one

Exercise 1

Ask Student A for clues and fill in Crossword puzzle 1. In each clue, the "blank" in Student A's sentence is the answer.

Crossword puzzle 1

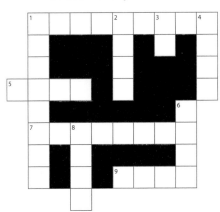

Example	
Student B	What's 1 down?
Student A	I "blank" with you. I think cats are smarter than dogs.
Student B	Disagree?
Student A	That's right!

Exercise 2

Give Student A clues for each answer in Crossword puzzle 2 until Student A guesses the answer. Use "blanks" in your clues. (You can give more than one clue for an answer.)

Memo

For help with clues, you can look at the unit shown for each word, but try to make up your own sentences.

Example	
Student A	What's 1 down?
Student B	He's poor now, but I'm sure he'll be rich "blank."
Student A	Someday?
Student B	That's right!

Unit: 14 Making predictions
Unit 2: Describing things
Unit 11: Giving advice and making suggestions
Unit 1: Asking for information
Unit 3: Making requests

Crossword puzzle 2

Unit 3: Making requests
Unit 4: Giving instructions
Getting Started: Personal information

Unit 11: Giving advice and making suggestions

Unit 14: Making predictions

S			C	O	U	L	D		P
H	O	W			U				O
M		L	A	N	G	U	A	G	E	S
E		E			H				S
D		A			T		C		I
M	A	T	T	E	R		O		B
Y		H					S		L
D	E	F	I	N	I	T	E	L	Y
R						S		

Player, turn to page 87

Caller

Language game

| Exercise 1 | Do this exercise alone. |

Look through the book for ideas and write ten questions and answers side by side in the blanks below. Then number the questions and answers below from 1 to 20 in *random order* (all mixed up).

| Example |

Question

⑪ Can I close the door?

Answer

④ Sure, go ahead.

Memo

- Exercise 1 may be assigned as homework.
- Important: make sure that each answer *cannot* be used with any other question.
- The teacher should check your sentences before Exercise 2.

| Exercise 2 | Play this game with two to four "players" (page 87) and one "caller." |

The players will take turns choosing two numbers. Listen for the first number and read the first sentence. Listen for the second number, read the second sentence and say if it matches the first sentence or not.* After that, the next player chooses.

Continue until all the questions and answers are matched. The player with the most matches wins!

*You can also ask the players if it is a match before you tell them.

Question

Answer

○ ○
○ ○
○ ○
○ ○
○ ○
○ ○
○ ○
○ ○
○ ○
○ ○

Self-study exercises

Exercise 1 1–4

Memo
Write the number of the conversation next to the sentence.

Listen to each conversation (1–4) and choose the best sentence to come *before* the first line of the conversation.

◻ The final showing starts at eight thirty.

◻ So, is that time good for you?

◻ I'm sorry, but we don't have it right now.

◻ Parts will be about two eighty, and labor about one twenty.

Exercise 2 5–8

Listen to each conversation (1–4) again and choose the best sentence to come *after* the last line of the conversation.

◻ Could I have your name, please?

◻ No, that's OK. We'll call you if there's a problem.

◻ See you then. Goodbye.

◻ No problem. Have a good day.

 **Self-study exercises**

Exercise 1

Listen to the conversations (1–6) and write "T" (true) or "F" (false) next to each sentence.

Conversation one 9

☐ The woman lost a black bag.

☐ The woman lost her bag at around ten o'clock.

Conversation two 10

☐ The girls received something from their father.

☐ The first girl does not like it.

Conversation three 11

☐ The women's bags are similar.

☐ The main difference is the size.

Conversation four 12

☐ It is the boy's birthday today.

☐ The boy knows what his present is.

Conversation five 13

☐ The man wants one made only of real leather.

☐ The man wants one with only key locks.

Conversation six 14

☐ The woman's camera was stolen yesterday.

☐ The woman's camera is black.

Exercise 2

Rewrite the false sentences to make them true.

Self-study exercises

Exercise 1 15

Listen to the conversation and check (✓) the five questions that *can* be answered. Then listen again and write the answers to the five questions.

☐ Where does Julie ask Alex to take her?

☐ What does Julie need to buy?

☐ How much money does Julie want?

☐ How many people does Julie ask Alex to pick up?

☐ What is the English homework on?

☐ Who does Julie ask Alex to watch?

☐ What is Alex going to do tomorrow afternoon?

☐ What time·does the party start?

Exercise 2 16

Rewrite these sentences from the conversation in the correct order. Then listen and check your answers.

> **Memo**
> Add punctuation and use capital letters where necessary.

1 but I have / this weekend / things to do / yeah / a million

_____

2 but / well / a small car / I'd be glad to / it's

_____

3 Math homework / you mind / but / checking / would / my

_____

4 how can I / the party / if you can't / for me / but / get ready for / do anything

_____

Self-study exercises

Exercise 1

Listen to the conversations (1–3). Find the differences in each conversation below.

Conversation one 17

Wife	Excuse me, miss? How can I turn off my reading light?
Flight attendant	Just press this button here, in your armrest … the one with the little light bulb on it.
Wife	Oh yes, I see. Thanks.

Conversation two 18

Husband	Excuse me, ma'am, but could you tell me how to use these headphones?
Flight attendant	Sure, just put them in here … that's right, and push the red buttons to adjust the volume, and push the blue buttons to change the channel.
Husband	OK, I have it now. Thanks a lot.

Conversation three 19

Flight attendant	Would you care for a blanket or a pillow?
Wife	Not right now, thank you. Maybe later.
Flight attendant	OK. If you need to call me for something, just press this button with the little figure on it.
Wife	Oh, this one next to the light button? Thank you very much.

Exercise 2

Listen to the conversations (4–6). Fill in the missing words.

Conversation four 20

Flight attendant	We're serving dinner now, ma'am. Could you pull your _____ down, please?
Wife	Oh yes, um, just a _____
Flight attendant	First, just pull that lever out and _____ it, and then pull the tray down.
Wife	Yes, of _____ , there.

Conversation five 21

Husband	Excuse me, how can I adjust my _____
Flight attendant	OK, first you press this _____ button on your armrest and hold it. Then you just push back against the seat or _____ forward.
Husband	I see, thank you.

Conversation six  22

Wife	Is this the air control up _____
Husband	I don't know. _____ me ma'am, is this the air control?
Flight attendant	Yes, it is. Turn it _____ to open it, and to close it, turn it counterclockwise.

Self-study exercises

www.fifty-fifty-series.com

Exercise 1

Listen to each conversation (1 and 2) and check (✓) the best sentence to come *before* the first line of the conversation.

Conversation one 23

☐ How are you today?	☐ Come on in and have a seat.
☐ Would you like a drink?	☐ Let's sit outside.

Conversation two 24

☐ I think you forgot something.	☐ Did your mother say it was OK?
☐ What do you need, son?	☐ Keep it down, I'm on the phone.

Exercise 2

Listen to each conversation (1 and 2) again and check (✓) the best sentence to come *after* the last line of the conversation.

Conversation one 25

☐ Do you have an ashtray?	☐ I'll see you later then.
☐ I'll just go outside.	☐ In that case, never mind.

Conversation two 26

☐ Is there gas in it?	☐ Come on, Dad, I'll be careful.
☐ Thanks, Dad, you're the best.	☐ OK. I'll be home by eleven.

Self-study exercise

 27

Listen to the conversation and choose the best answer to each question.

1 What is this conversation mainly about?

  a. Jonathan's homework
  b. Jonathan's sore foot
  c. Jonathan's behavior
  d. Jonathan's next class

2 Why does Mrs. Fenway ask to see Jonathan?

  a. He received a low grade.
  b. He did not do his homework.
  c. He was disruptive in class.
  d. He had a family problem.

3 What is Jonathan's excuse for not doing his homework?

  a. He lost the book.
  b. He was sick.
  c. He read the wrong chapter.
  d. He forgot.

4 Why didn't Jonathan do his homework really?

  a. He watched TV instead.
  b. He fell asleep.
  c. He had too much other homework.
  d. He found it too difficult.

5 What does Jonathan do when he leaves the classroom?

  a. He shouts to his friends.
  b. He runs in the hallway.
  c. He laughs at the teacher.
  d. He goes the wrong way.

6 Mrs. Fenway thinks Jonathan is _____ .

  a. funny
  b. good-hearted
  c. naughty
  d. unlucky

8 Self-study exercises

Exercise 1 28

Listen to the conversation and check (✓) the five questions that *can* be answered. Then listen again and write the answers to the five questions.

☐	What does John want to build?	
☐	How much food is there?	
☐	What does Rob want to build?	
☐	What tools do they have?	
☐	Who is the strongest?	
☐	How many people does Megan think should go for help?	
☐	What does John think of Megan's plan?	
☐	Where are the four speakers?	

Exercise 2 29

Rewrite these sentences from the conversation in the correct order. Then listen and check your answers.

Memo
Add punctuation and use capital letters where necessary.

1 sure / for us / I'm / they're / looking / already

_____

2 get out / ourselves / we have to / Rob / of here

_____

3 we're / I / here / believe / safe / all

_____

4 should / in / all / my opinion / stick / we / together

_____

 **Self-study exercises**

Exercise 1 30–34

Listen to each conversation (1–5) and choose the best sentence to come *before* the first line of the conversation.

☐ Look, I've almost finished.	☐ How do they feel?
☐ I really need to get away.	☐ I think I like the red one.
☐ Look at those two over there.	

Exercise 2 35–39

Listen to each conversation (1–5) again and choose the best sentence to come *after* the last line of the conversation.

☐ An excellent choice.	☐ Well, it's up to you.
☐ You look great.	☐ I guess that's long enough.
☐ Yes, I suppose we will.	

Self-study exercise

 40

Listen to the conversation and choose the best answer to each question.

1 What is this conversation mainly about?

  a. George's DJ friend

  b. a graduation party

  c. office gossip

  d. the price of party tents

2 Sophie is probably Elizabeth's _____ .

  a. friend

  b. student

  c. daughter

  d. niece

3 Why doesn't Elizabeth want a live band?

  a. They are too noisy.

  b. They are old-fashioned.

  c. They are expensive and a lot of trouble.

  d. They are expensive and too noisy.

4 What kind of weather is Elizabeth worried about?

  a. rain

  b. snow

  c. fog

  d. sun

5 What does Elizabeth think of Jenny's ideas?

  a. They sound too expensive.

  b. Some are good and some are bad.

  c. She needs more time to think about them.

  d. They are great.

6 Elizabeth thinks George's suggestions are _____ .

  a. helpful

  b. extravagant

  c. creative

  d. boring

Self-study exercises

Exercise 1 41

Listen to the conversation and check (✓) the five questions that *can* be answered. Then listen again and write the answers to the five questions.

When did the accident at the intersection happen?

How did the accident at the intersection happen?

When did Linda have a bad car accident?

Who was in the car with Linda?

What pushed them against a wall?

Who was hurt?

What did the truck driver say?

How much did the car repair cost?

Exercise 2  42

Rewrite these sentences from the conversation in the correct order. Then listen and check your answers.

> **Memo**
>
> Add punctuation and use capital letters where necessary.

1 a bad / Linda / have you / car accident / ever had

_____

2 stopped / we came / the right lane / to a red light / and / in

_____

3 had to / through / climb out / we / the broken / windshield

_____

4 I've / anyway / like this one / since then / real careful / always been / of trucks

_____

Self-study exercise

 43

Listen to the conversation and choose the best answer to each question.

1 What is the main purpose of this conversation?

  a. to find out about French class

  b. to schedule a date

  c. to share funny stories

  d. to impress Mia

2 What is Mia doing on Friday night?

  a. watching TV at a friend's house

  b. going swimming

  c. going to a movie

  d. going to a birthday party

3 When is Mia free?

  a. on Saturday morning

  b. on Saturday afternoon

  c. on Sunday morning

  d. on Sunday night

4 What is Zachary doing on Sunday night?

  a. having dinner with Mia

  b. taking a friend to the airport

  c. seeing his family

  d. nothing

5 Mia is _____ that Zachary is busy.

  a. unconcerned

  b. heartbroken

  c. relieved

  d. frustrated

6 How does Zachary feel about Mia?

  a. He doesn't think she is that special.

  b. He thinks she is all right.

  c. He is slightly interested in her.

  d. He likes her a lot.

Self-study exercises

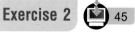

 Self-study exercises (side text)

Exercise 1 44

Listen to the conversation and check (✓) the five questions that *can* be answered. Then listen again and write the answers to the five questions.

☐ What time do they have to go to the airport?

☐ Where is Harry going?

☐ What's wrong with Loni?

☐ What is Harry's new job?

☐ Where did Harry learn Japanese?

☐ When will Jack and Loni see Harry again?

☐ How will the family keep in touch?

☐ What will Jack and Loni do if Harry doesn't come back?

Exercise 2 45

Rewrite these sentences from the conversation in the correct order. Then listen and check your answers.

Memo

Add punctuation and use capital letters where necessary.

1 out / right now / friends / he's / with

_____

2 he's going to / I'm sure / a great time / have

_____

3 quickly / the time / pass / probably / very / will

_____

4 a family / he / have / over there / might meet / and / a girl

_____

114

SELF-STUDY EXERCISES ANSWER KEY

UNIT ❶

Exercise 1

4   1

2   3

Exercise 2

2   3

1   4

UNIT ❷

Conversation one

[F] The woman lost a brown bag.

[T]

Conversation two

[T]

[F] The first girl thinks it is awesome.

Conversation three

[T]

[F] The main difference is the strap.

Conversation four

[F] It is the boy's birthday tomorrow.

[T]

Conversation five

[T]

[F] The man wants one with either key locks or combination locks.

Conversation six

[F] The woman's camera was stolen just a minute ago.

[T]

UNIT ❸

Exercise 1

[✓] Julie asks Alex to take her shopping.

[ ]

[✓] Julie wants thirty or forty dollars.

[✓] Julie asks Alex to pick up five people.

[ ]

[✓] Julie asks Alex to watch her brother Jimmy.

[✓] Alex is going to go to basketball practice tomorrow afternoon.

[ ]

Exercise 2

1 Yeah, but I have a million things to do this weekend.

2 Well, it's a small car, but I'd be glad to.

3 But would you mind checking my Math homework?

4 But how can I get ready for the party if you can't do anything for me?

UNIT ❹

Exercise 1

Conversation one

Wife	Excuse me, miss? How can I turn ~~off~~ my reading light? on
Flight attendant	Just ~~press~~ this button here, push in your armrest … the one with the little light bulb on it.
Wife	Oh yes, I see. ~~Thanks~~. Thank you

Conversation two

Husband	~~Excuse~~ me, ma'am, but could Pardon you tell me how to use these headphones?
Flight attendant	Sure, just ~~put~~ them in here … plug that's right, and push the red buttons to adjust the volume, and push the blue buttons to change the channel.
Husband	OK, I have it now. ~~Thanks a lot~~. Thank you very much

Conversation three

Flight attendant	Would you ~~care for~~ a blanket like or a pillow?
Wife	Not right now, thank you. Maybe later.
Flight attendant	OK. If you need to call me for ~~something~~, just press this anything button with the little figure on it.
Wife	Oh, this one ~~next to~~ to the light by button? Thank you very much.

Exercise 2

Conversation four

Flight attendant	We're serving dinner now, ma'am. Could you pull your <u>tray</u> down, please?
Wife	Oh yes, um, just a <u>second …</u>
Flight attendant	First, just pull that lever out and <u>turn</u> it, and then pull the tray down.
Wife	Yes, of <u>course</u> , there.

Conversation five

Husband	Excuse me, how can I adjust my <u>seat</u>?
Flight attendant	OK, first you press this <u>large</u> button on your armrest and hold it. Then you just push back against the seat or <u>lean</u> forward.
Husband	I see, thank you.

Conversation six

Wife	Is this the air control up <u>here?</u>
Husband	I don't know. <u>Excuse</u> me ma'am, is this the air control?
Flight attendant	Yes, it is. Turn it <u>clockwise</u> to open it, and to close it, turn it counterclockwise.

UNIT ⑥

Exercise 1

Conversation one

☐   ☑
☐   ☐

Conversation two

☐   ☐
☑   ☐

Exercise 2

Conversation one

☑   ☐
☐   ☐

Conversation two

☐   ☑
☐   ☐

UNIT ⑦

1	c	**3**	c	**5**	b
2	b	**4**	a	**6**	c

UNIT ⑧

Exercise 1

☑ John wants to build a raft.
☑ There is plenty of food.
☑ Rob wants to build a shelter.
☐
☐
☑ Megan thinks just one person should go for help.
☑ John thinks Megan's plan is too dangerous.
☐

Exercise 2

1 I'm sure they're already looking for us …
2 We have to get out of here ourselves, Rob.
3 I believe we're all safe here.
4 In my opinion we should all stick together.

UNIT ⑨

Exercise 1

⑤   ①
④   ②
③

Exercise 2

①   ②
③   ④
⑤

UNIT ⑪

1	b	**3**	c	**5**	d
2	c	**4**	a	**6**	b

UNIT ⑫

Exercise 1

☑ The accident happened last week.
☐
☑ Linda had a bad car accident a long time ago.
☑ A friend was in the car with Linda.
☑ A really big truck pushed them against a wall.
☑ No one was hurt.
☐
☐

Exercise 2

1 Have you ever had a bad car accident, Linda?
2 We came to a red light and stopped in the right lane.
3 We had to climb out through the broken windshield.
4 Anyway, since then I've always been real careful of trucks, like this one.

UNIT ⑬

1	b	**3**	d	**5**	a
2	a	**4**	b	**6**	d

UNIT ⑭

Exercise 1

☑ They have to go to the airport at six in the morning.
☑ Harry is going to Japan.
☑ Loni is nervous about Harry's trip to Japan.
☐
☐
☑ They will see him in one year.
☐
☑ They will visit him in Japan.

Exercise 2

1 He's out with friends right now.
2 I'm sure he's going to have a great time.
3 The time will probably pass very quickly.
4 He might meet a girl and have a family over there!

Audio Script

GETTING STARTED

Listening task, page 3

John	Nice party, huh?
Maria	Yeah, it is. Jack has a lot of friends.
John	Right, and a big family, too. I'm John, by the way, John Fletcher.
Maria	Hi, I'm Maria Gomez. So, are you a friend or family?
John	A friend. We play tennis together. But I know Jack from our college days, out in L.A.
Maria	Oh, really? So, where are you from?
John	Denver, originally, but I live here in Chicago now. And you?
Maria	Oh, I grew up here, and I live down the street.
John	So, how do you know Jack, Maria?
Maria	We teach at the same school. I'm an art teacher.
John	That's interesting. I'm a graphic designer. Magazine work.
Maria	Really? So, you're interested in art …
John	Oh, yeah, very much. I love going to shows.
Maria	Me, too.
John	Oh, yeah? Have you seen the Picasso exhibit at the Art Institute yet?
Maria	No, but—
John	Listen, I'm going there tomorrow with Jack and a few friends. You probably know them. Would you like to go with us?
Maria	Sure, I'd love to.
John	Terrific. Let me tell you who's going …

UNIT ❶

Listening task, page 6

Conversation one

Woman	Sure, Thursday at four is fine. Could you tell me about how long my visit will be? … I see, OK. Do you know if I'll be able to eat afterwards? … Right, OK, I didn't think so. OK, see you Thursday … Bye-bye.

Conversation two

Woman	OK, I guess I'll just have to order it … Well, do you know how long it'll take if I order it now? … Two weeks, OK, and do I have to pay for it first, or — When I pick it up, I see … OK, I guess I *will* order it now.

Conversation three

Woman	Four hundred dollars?! I thought it was going to cost about two fifty! … Yeah, I know, I know, but could you tell me what costs so much? … Uh huh … OK, I see. So, it'll be ready by Friday morning. OK, should I call first to make sure it's all done?

Conversation four

Woman	And could you tell me what time it's over? … Oh, that late? OK. Oh, one more thing, do we have to get there early? I mean, do you know if there'll be a long line? … No? Great, thank you very much.

UNIT ❷

Listening task, page 11

Conversation one

Clerk	I understand, miss, but we have a few of those. Can you tell me what it looks like?
Woman	Well, it's very plain, with almost no design, and it's made of leather—soft brown leather. And it doesn't have a strap or zipper, just one little gold snap. It's a little larger than pocket-size.
Clerk	I'm sorry, you said it's brown?
Woman	Right. I lost it around ten o'clock this morning.
Clerk	OK, just a minute, I'll see if we have it.

Conversation two

Girl 1	Yeah, it came this morning. Daddy *told* us he'd send one.
Girl 2	Is it a nice one? What does it look like?
Girl 1	It's mostly black, and it has a beautiful design all around it. And it has a neat little silver latch and little silver plates on the corners. It's awesome!

Conversation three

Woman 1	Where did you get that? It looks just like mine!
Woman 2	Really? I bought it in Mexico. Is it the same as yours?
Woman 1	Well, almost. Mine is made of leather, too, and it's the same size, but it has a longer, thinner strap.
Woman 2	Does it have these little leather strings on the front?
Woman 1	Yeah, two, just like that.

Conversation four

Boy	Come on, Dad, tell me! What's in the box?
Dad	Your birthday is *tomorrow*, Shawn.
Boy	OK, just tell me what it looks like … please?
Dad	Well, it's small, and it's mostly made of plastic, and it has a little screen, and—
Boy	Does it have earphones?
Dad	OK, I give up. Go ahead and open it.

Conversation five

Man 1	So, can you buy one for me while you're there?
Man 2	Yeah, sure, but there are so many types. What kind do you want?
Man 1	You know, just a plain brown one, made of *real* leather, of course. And I like the ones with locks on the latches.
Man 2	Key locks or combination locks?
Man 1	Either is OK.

Conversation six

Woman	It happened just a minute ago! This guy sat next to me, then got up and left in a hurry, and now it's gone!
Police officer	Please, ma'am, calm down. What does it look like?
Woman	Well, you know, it's black, and it has a thin, black shoulder strap. It's not in a case or anything. Please hurry, officer! He'll get away!
Police officer	What did the guy look like?

UNIT ❸

Listening task, page 16

Alex	It's going to be a great party on Sunday, huh Julie?
Julie	Yeah, but I have a *million* things to do this weekend.
Alex	Is there anything I can do?
Julie	Well, yeah, maybe. Do you think you could take me shopping tonight?
Alex	I guess so. I'm going to—
Julie	Listen, can you lend me thirty or forty dollars?
Alex	No problem. I have about sixty, but I need to—
Julie	OK. Later, could you possibly pick up Gina and Marisol and Bonnie and Amanda and Michelle?

Alex	Well, it's a small car, but I'd be glad to. I'm—
Julie	And listen, I don't have time to do that English homework, so I was wondering if you could possibly write a page or two for me?
Alex	I wish I could, but I really have a lot of homework, and—
Julie	OK, OK, never mind. But would you mind checking my Math homework?
Alex	Not at all. Tonight I have to do *my* Math homework, and—
Julie	Are you free tomorrow?
Alex	Tomorrow?
Julie	Yeah. Would it be possible for you to watch my brother Jimmy for an hour or two? I'm supposed to babysit after lunch, but—
Alex	I'm afraid I have basketball practice all afternoon, and—
Julie	Basketball practice? But how can I get ready for the party if you can't *do* anything for me?

UNIT ❹

Listening task, page 22

Exercise 1

Conversation one

Wife	Excuse me, miss? How can I turn on my reading light?
Flight attendant	Just push this button here, in your armrest … the one with the little light bulb on it.
Wife	Oh yes, I see. Thank you.

Conversation two

Husband	Pardon me, ma'am, but could you tell me how to use these headphones?
Flight attendant	Sure, just plug them in here … that's right, and push the red buttons to adjust the volume, and push the blue buttons to change the channel.
Husband	OK, I have it now. Thank you very much.

Conversation three

Flight attendant	Would you like a blanket or a pillow?
Wife	Not right now, thank you. Maybe later.

Flight attendant	OK. If you need to call me for anything, just press this button with the little figure on it.
Wife	Oh, this one by the light button? Thank you very much.

Conversation four

Flight attendant	We're serving dinner now, ma'am. Could you pull your tray down, please?
Wife	Oh yes, um, just a second …
Flight attendant	First, just pull that lever out and turn it, and then pull the tray down.
Wife	Yes, of course, there.

Conversation five

Husband	Excuse me, how can I adjust my seat?
Flight attendant	OK, first you press this large button on your armrest and hold it. Then you just push back against the seat or lean forward.
Husband	I see, thank you.

Conversation six

Wife	Is this the air control up here?
Husband	I don't know. Excuse me ma'am, is this the air control?
Flight attendant	Yes, it is. Turn it clockwise to open it, and to close it, turn it counterclockwise.

Exercise 2

Conversation one

Wife	Where is that light switch again?
Husband	Um, let's see … Push that thing up there next to the light.
Wife	I thought I had to push a button in the armrest here.
Husband	No, I think it's up there, next to the light.

Conversation two

Husband	That's right, dear, just plug them in there, then push the red buttons to adjust the volume, and—
Wife	Don't I push the blue buttons to adjust the volume?
Husband	No, she said push the red buttons for the volume! Push the *blue* buttons to change the channel!

Conversation three

Husband	I push this button with the light bulb to call the flight attendant, right?
Wife	No, not that button. Push the other button.
Husband	What other button? I thought it was this button with the little light to call her …
Wife	No, no, push that button *next* to the light button to call her.

Conversation four

Husband	I can't get this food tray out!
Wife	Just turn the lever and pull the tray down, dear.
Husband	No, no, you pull the lever first and then turn it to get the tray out. See?

Conversation five

Husband	This seat won't go back!
Wife	Just press that large button and—
Husband	I *did* press it!
Wife	And hold it in.
Husband	What? No, you don't have to hold it in.

Conversation six

Wife	Dear, could you turn that air control thingamajig clockwise for me?
Husband	You want it closed?
Wife	No, open.
Husband	Well, to open it you turn it *counter*clockwise.
Wife	Clockwise!
Husband	Counterclockwise!
Wife	Would you just turn it clockwise!

UNIT 5

Listening task, page 28

Conversation one

Sister	Could you do this? I want to go shopping.
Brother	Well, OK. But can you tell me how to use this?
Sister	When everything is in make sure the door is closed tight. Then pour one cup in the compartment in the top. It's that larger one on the left.
Brother	This one?
Sister	Yeah, and turn this dial to "hot." Here, I got it.
Brother	That's it?
Sister	Do you have quarters?
Brother	Ummm … no.

Conversation two

Woman	Excuse me, can you tell me what this is made of?
Salesperson	Let me see. Yes, the outside is sixty-five percent polyester and thirty-five percent cotton, and the lining is made of one hundred percent nylon. The filling is one hundred percent down.
Woman	Do you know if it has a hood?
Salesperson	Let me see. Yes, just unzip the back of the collar and pull it out.

Conversation three

Mark	Excuse me, but I'm new here, and—
Nina	No wonder I've never seen you before.
Mark	Yeah, well, do you know how to—
Nina	My name is Nina, by the way.
Mark	Hi, Nina. I'm Mark, nice to meet you. Anyway, could you tell me how to use this? I've never—
Nina	Oh, sure. Just put your page in here, face down, dial the number and press this button here.
Mark	I see, thanks.
Nina	Anytime. Um, Mark, do you know how to use the copier?

Conversation four

Allison	Shawn, can you get my ski jacket and wool scarf for me?
Shawn	Sure … um, could you tell me what the jacket looks like? There are a dozen in here.
Allison	Oh, well, the jacket is light blue, and it has a white lining, and the scarf has blue and white stripes.
Shawn	Oh, yeah, I got them … I think.
Allison	And could you see if my sunglasses are in the inside pocket?
Shawn	This one doesn't *have* an inside pocket, Allison.

Conversation five

Woman	I'm looking for something small and light.
Salesperson	Ah, small and light. Well, this one is popular. It has all the necessary attachments.
Woman	I don't know. How do you empty it?
Salesperson	Just press this button here, remove the front cover and take out the bag. Then just slip a new bag in and close the cover.
Woman	Is this the only color? I hate gray.

Salesperson	Ah, you hate gray. Could you wait just a minute while I check?
Woman	Is this going to take long? I have to go.

UNIT

Listening task, page 33

Conversation one

Friend 1	Mind if I smoke in here?
Friend 2	No, go ahead.

Conversation two

Son	Is it OK if I use the new car tonight, Dad?
Dad	I'd rather you didn't.

Conversation three

Friend 1	Could I possibly use your phone?
Friend 2	Sorry, but the battery's low.

Conversation four

Brother	Hey, Sis! Do you mind if I borrow your laptop computer this weekend? I have a lot of homework to do.
Sister	Afraid not. I have a lot of homework to do, too.

Conversation five

Girl	Can I go to a party Saturday night with Susan and Jenny?
Mom	Uh huh. Don't be late.

Conversation six

Friend 1	Is it all right if I open this window?
Friend 2	Of course.

Conversation seven

Friend 1	Mind if I turn off the TV? Nobody's watching it.
Friend 2	Not at all.

Conversation eight

Man	Excuse me, Mr. Bellows. Would it be possible for me to take next Monday off? I have to take my sister home from the hospital.
Boss	Uh huh. That'll be fine.

Conversation nine

Man 1	Hey, is it OK if I park here for a minute?
Man 2	No problem.

Conversation ten

Student	Mr. Riley, is it OK if I leave the room? I have to go to my locker.
Teacher	Go ahead.

UNIT 7

Listening task, page 39

Mrs. Fenway	And don't forget to read Chapter Five and answer the questions on page ninety-nine! Oh, Jonathan, just a minute … I want to speak to you.
Jonathan	Yes, Mrs. Fenway?
Mrs. Fenway	Jonathan, why didn't you answer any questions on the homework sheet?
Jonathan	Oh, I'm sorry Mrs. Fenway, but I read the wrong chapter last night.
Mrs. Fenway	Oh, I see. But why didn't you read the right chapter after you looked at the questions?
Jonathan	Well, I had to do too much *other* homework.
Mrs. Fenway	Now, Jonathan, you didn't have that much homework. You have to stop watching TV.
Jonathan	Yes, Mrs. Fenway.
Mrs. Fenway	And why were you late this morning?
Jonathan	Oh, I had to walk to school because … because the school bus got a flat tire.
Mrs. Fenway	A flat tire? Come on, Jonathan, no other students were late today.
Jonathan	Yeah, well, I couldn't walk fast because I have a sore foot.
Mrs. Fenway	Ah, a sore foot. Well, you'd better get to your next class or you'll be late again.
Jonathan	OK, Mrs. Fenway. See you tomorrow.
Mrs. Fenway	Jonathan!
Jonathan	Yes?
Mrs. Fenway	Do not run in the hallway.
Jonathan	Sorry.

UNIT 8

Listening task, page 44

Rob	Somebody will find us. I'm sure they're already looking for us … They'll find us, right John?
John	I don't know, Rob. They may never find us. I think we should build a raft and the four of us should sail out of here.
Emma	I agree with John. We have to get out of here ourselves, Rob.
Rob	I don't think so, Emma. I believe we're all safe here. There's plenty of food and water. In my opinion we should build a shelter and wait to be rescued. What do you think, Megan?
Megan	I disagree with you, Rob. We can't wait forever. We have to do something, but I think that just one of us should try to get help, and the rest stay here.
John	Actually, Megan, I think that it's too dangerous out there for one person …
Rob	Right, John, I think so too. In my opinion we should all stick together.
Emma	That's true, but we can't just sit here!
Megan	I agree completely, Emma … Well then, I guess we should all go together, like John says …
Emma	Absolutely! Let's make a raft!

UNIT 9

Listening task, page 50

Conversation one

Man	I like the style, but I'm not sure about the fit. Do you have a bigger size?
Salesperson	Just a moment. Ah, yes. Would you like to try the white ones? They're bigger.
Man	Sure, thanks. Oh yeah, these are much more comfortable. I'll take them.

Conversation two

Man	You want the red one, huh?
Woman	Yeah. It's roomier than the blue one.
Man	Well, yes, but it's not as sporty as the blue one.
Woman	That's true, but the red one's better for shopping and things like that.

Conversation three

Lisa	They're cute, aren't they? Which one do you like, Janet?
Janet	The one on the right, I think. He's much more handsome.
Lisa	Do you think so? I like the other one. He looks more mature. And taller!
Janet	Look, they're coming over, Lisa! Quick, how do I look?

Conversation four 54

Travel agent	How long do you have in mind?
Woman	I'm not sure. Could you give me some idea of the prices?
Travel agent	Sure. Let's see, the five-island cruise is ten days … That's two thousand dollars.
Woman	Do you have anything cheaper?
Travel agent	Yes, of course. This three-island cruise is only one thousand five hundred dollars, but it's shorter. It's only seven days.

Conversation five 55

Woman	Oh, yours is much better than mine!
Man	No, not at all. I think yours is as nice as mine.
Woman	No, no, no, not really. Yours is beautiful. Mine is not nearly as colorful.
Man	Oh, well, thank you. Oh, look at the time.
Woman	Oh, my, I think we'll have to finish them tomorrow.

UNIT 10

Listening task, page 56

Conversation one 56

Man	In my opinion, Paris is much more expensive than New York.
Woman	I couldn't agree more, but a nice apartment does cost a bit more in New York.
Man	That's true, but everything else, like food, entertainment, transportation—
Woman	Absolutely, especially if you have a car. By the way, did you drive here today?
Man	As a matter of fact I did. My car is right over there. Would you like a ride home later?
Woman	I'd love a ride home, thank you.

Conversation two 57

Husband	I don't know, this is much more expensive than a bicycle. What do you think?
Wife	I think he'd enjoy the car more at first, but actually, he'll use the bicycle a lot more.
Husband	Yeah, I think so, too. We can get the bike *and* something else with the extra money.
Wife	That's true. Let's go and look at bikes, and then at jewelry.
Husband	OK, but first I want to look at tools.
Wife	No, jewelry first.

Conversation three 58

Angela	Justin, how did you *do* that?
Justin	It wasn't my fault! A kid on a bicycle shot into the street, and I went up the sidewalk and hit a telephone pole.
Angela	If you ask me, Dad is going to kill you!
Justin	No he won't. I'm going to get it fixed like new.
Angela	How much do you think it's going to cost?
Justin	I don't think it'll be more than five hundred dollars. So could you lend me two hundred dollars, Angela?
Angela	Yeah, right!
Justin	Come on, Angela, Dad is going to kill me!

Conversation four 59

Simon	But Mom, why can't I get a motorcycle? Lots of kids in high school have motorcycles, and they're cheaper than cars …
Mom	Simon, I don't care about other kids. Motorcycles are far more dangerous than cars, and you are still a new driver.
Simon	But motorcycles are more fun, and they're easier to park and much better on gas.
Mom	What does your father think?
Simon	Well … He said no. But if you—
Mom	I agree with your father completely. Here he comes. Put that away.

Conversation five 60

Miss Lee	Joshua, I didn't see you at rehearsal yesterday. Where were you?
Joshua	I'm sorry, Miss Lee, but my brother needed help fixing his car. I had to go straight home yesterday.
Miss Lee	Well, don't miss it this afternoon, OK?
Joshua	I won't, I promise. But Miss Lee, I was wondering if I could hand in the final paper a few days late. I have to go shopping with my sister this weekend.
Miss Lee	Well, OK, but no later than Wednesday, and don't miss any more rehearsals. The school play is next week, Romeo.

UNIT 11

Listening task, page 62 62

Jenny	So, Elizabeth, what are you going to do for Sophie's graduation party?
Elizabeth	I don't know, Jenny … any ideas?
George	Why don't you rent a limousine to bring her to the party?
Elizabeth	A limo? I don't think so, George.

Jenny	You ought to rent one of those huge widescreen TVs and play music videos.
Elizabeth	Music videos … That sounds good, yeah.
George	And a band, Liz, you should get a live band! I know these guys—
Elizabeth	Um, that sounds interesting George, but that's a little expensive and a lot of trouble.
George	Oh. Then, how about a disc jockey? I know this guy, and he's not expensive …
Elizabeth	Hmmm … Yeah, that might be better. Music videos *inside* and a DJ *outside* … Let me think about it.
Jenny	Listen, why don't you have fireworks in the evening?
Elizabeth	Good idea, Jenny! Sophie loves fireworks! I hope it doesn't rain.
George	Maybe you'd better rent one of those big party tents.
Elizabeth	That *is* a good idea, George, but first I'll have to check the price and the size of the tent.
Jenny	And if I were you, Elizabeth, I'd hire caterers to cook and serve the food.
Elizabeth	Caterers … Yeah, that sounds like a good idea, too.
George	I know! How about Hawaiian hula dancers serving the food, and … Hey, where are you going?

UNIT 12

Listening task, page 68 64

Janet	Did you hear about the accident at this intersection last week?
Linda	Yeah, I saw it on TV. Pretty bad.
Janet	Have you ever had a bad car accident, Linda?
Linda	Yeah, a long time ago.
Janet	Really? What happened?
Linda	Well, I was driving with a friend in the city. We came to a red light and stopped in the right lane. There was a wall next to us, on the right. A really big truck pulled up next to us on the left.
Janet	Yeah?
Linda	The light changed green, we started off, and the truck moved over to the right.
Janet	Oh, no.
Linda	It pushed my car against the wall. He just didn't see me!
Janet	Wow! Was anyone hurt?
Linda	No, we were really lucky … just scratched from broken glass. All the windows broke. When we stopped, we were against the wall on the right, and the truck was against us on the left.

Janet	You couldn't get out?
Linda	No! We had to climb out through the broken windshield.
Janet	Gee, you *were* lucky. You could've been killed!
Linda	Yeah. Anyway, since then I've always been real careful of trucks, like this one.
Janet	Yeah, right, and walls like that.
Linda and Janet	Uh-oh!

UNIT 13

Listening task, page 74   66

Mia	Hello?
Zachary	Hello, Mia? This is Zachary.
Mia	Oh, hi, Zachary, what's up?
Zachary	Oh, nothing much. Are you busy this weekend?
Mia	Well, sort of. Why?
Zachary	Would you like to see a movie Friday night?
Mia	I'd love to, Zachary, but I'm going to watch TV at Yuriko's house Friday night.
Zachary	Oh, I see, OK. Well how about going swimming Saturday afternoon?
Mia	I'm sorry, but I have a French class Saturday afternoon.
Zachary	Oh, I guess you're busy Saturday night, too, huh? I mean, do you feel like going bowling Saturday night?
Mia	That sounds great, Zachary, but I'm going to a birthday party for a girl in my French class. Sorry.
Zachary	Sunday night, Mia! Dinner! How about having dinner Sunday night? Or are you—
Mia	Sure, that's a great idea.
Zachary	What?
Mia	I said that's a great idea.
Zachary	Oh. Really?
Mia	Really. I'd love to.
Zachary	*Oh, no …*
Mia	What's the matter?
Zachary	Sunday night I have to take a friend to the airport …
Mia	Oh, well, maybe another time, then. Bye!

UNIT 14

Listening task, page 79 68

Jack	So, tell me, Loni, is Harry ready for his trip?
Loni	Yeah, he finished packing this evening. He's out with friends right now.
Jack	Well, we have to go to the airport at six in the morning, so … Hey, what's the matter?

Loni	Jack, I'm a little nervous about Harry's trip to Japan.
Jack	Come on, honey, he's twenty-two years old, it's a great job and he speaks a little Japanese. I'm sure he's going to have a great time.
Loni	But we won't see him for *one year*!
Jack	Don't worry. The time will probably pass very quickly.
Loni	But what if he stays there?
Jack	Stays there?
Loni	He might meet a girl and have a family over there!
Jack	So, what's wrong with that?
Loni	It's so far away.
Jack	He'll keep in touch.
Loni	I guess so, but—
Jack	But what?
Loni	Maybe he'll never come back!
Jack	Then we can visit him in Japan, OK?
Loni	Well, OK. Maybe we should learn Japanese, huh?
Jack	Good idea. *Arigato*.
Loni	Harry got two? Harry got two what?
Jack	No, no. "*Arigato*." That's "thank you" in Japanese. Harry taught me.

UNIT ⑮

Listening task, page 84

Conversation one 69

Man	So, how do you like it?
Woman	Well, it's OK so far, but … Have you ever been caught in a storm?
Man	No, not really. A little rain, maybe …
Woman	Well, I think there's going to be a storm. Look at that.
Man	Nah, it may rain a *little*, but I'm sure that there won't be a storm.
Woman	We are going to drown! We are definitely going to drown!
Man	Maybe we'd better get to shore …

Conversation two 70

George	Good morning, Jenny. Hey, you don't look so good. What's the matter?
Jenny	Oh, I feel awful! I have a terrible headache, and I'm so tired …
George	Why don't you go home early? I'm sure the boss will understand.
Jenny	Yeah, I know, but my desk will probably fill up with work while I'm out.

George	If I were you, I'd take it easy, relax and … Hey, I bought a trampoline last week! Why don't you come over after work, and—
Jenny	George, please, you've got to be kidding! Oh, my head …

Conversation three 71

Woman	I think I'd better—
Man	Dear, let me do this, OK?
Woman	But don't you think I should turn the water off first?
Man	I've fixed drains a dozen times before. Could you hand me that wrench?
Woman	OK, but it might leak.
Man	It'll be OK, could you just … Could, could you just turn off the water, please? Honey?! Hey, come back!

Conversation four 72

Woman	Let's do something different this weekend. We could go out. How about going to the beach?
Man	It's going to rain.
Woman	Oh, well, would you like to go Rollerblading?
Man	Nah, I've never gone Rollerblading before. I don't know how.
Woman	OK, then, do you feel like going to the movies?
Man	Nah. Hey, we haven't been to the video store in a while. Let's rent a few movies.
Woman	Different! I said something different!

Conversation five 73

Man	See? It's not so bad, right?
Woman	Listen, why don't we set up the tent?
Man	Come on, this will be great! Look at those stars!
Woman	I think we'll be eaten alive by mosquitoes. In fact, I think we'd better sleep in the car. Come on, move!
Man	OK, wait a minute. The door's locked. Could you give me the keys?
Woman	The keys? I don't have the keys! I thought *you* had the keys!